MW00668923

Make Your Mark in the Scriptures
–IN–
The Book of Mormon

Also by
Mark R. Hale

Make Your Mark in the Scriptures
—In—
The Doctrine and Covenants &
Pearl of Great Price

Make Your Mark in the Scriptures
—In—
The New Testament

Deje su marca en las escrituras
—en—
el Libro de Mormón

Make Your Mark in the Scriptures
–IN–
The Book of Mormon

Mark R. Hale

 ® Cobblemoor Lane
Books

Published by Hires Enterprises, Inc.
Salt Lake City, Utah

 Cobblemoor Lane
Books

8160 Highland Drive, Suite 210
Sandy, Utah 84093
cobblemoorlanebooks@gmail.com

Copyright 2007 by Mark R. Hale

All rights reserved. No part of this book may be reproduced in any form or by any means without permission in writing from the publisher, Hires Enterprises Inc., 8160 Highland Drive, Suite 210 Sandy, Utah 84093. This book is not an official publication of The Church of Jesus Christ of Latter-day Saints. The views expressed herein are the responsibility of the author and do not necessarily represent the position of the Church or of Hires Enterprises Inc.

Third Cobblemoor Lane Books Edition 2007

ISBN 0-9752890-8-X

Photography by Dana Sohm

Cover Design by Sam Morgan

This book is in tribute to my father and mother,
Don Hale and Shirley Hickman Hale,
who taught their children to be
wise as serpents and harmless as doves.

In appreciation of R. Scott Strong
who taught me that scripture scholarship is about making connections
between related scriptures;
and Marion M. Call for her excellent skills
in processing and editing.

Contents

Preface to the Third Edition

I recently read and reviewed every verse in the Book of Mormon to verify the color categories I initially selected for *Make Your Mark in the Scriptures -In- the Book of Mormon*. I have added additional colors to some verses indicating additional substance in these verses. I have also changed the colors for some verses indicating a switch in categories more accurately defining the substance of those verses. This third addition reflects these changes making this edition a stronger aid to gospel scholarship.

Introduction

Have you started reading the Book of Mormon many more times than you have finished it? And, once you have finished it, are you reluctant to start it again, chronologically, from beginning to end, Nephi to Moroni?

Have you said, "I think it's great that the Book of Mormon is 'the most correct of any book on earth, and the keystone of our religion, and a man would get nearer to God by abiding by its precepts, than by any other book'[1] but what does that mean, and what are those precepts?" Or have you asked the question, "Just what are the doctrines of the Book of Mormon, and where do I find them in the book?"

Have you vaguely recalled a scripture in the Book of Mormon that you really liked but could not find?

Have you been frustrated that, despite being a member of the Church your entire life, you still do not have a good handle on how to approach the Book of Mormon—how to read it, how to study it, and how to review it?

Have you sensed that you should be much more of a gospel student or gospel scholar in the Book of Mormon than you are—in light of all your personal reading in these scriptures and all of the Church classes you have attended over the years?

Have you felt that the Book of Mormon is so long and involved (a thousand year history) with so many chapters (239) that to approach it doctrinally appears almost unmanageable?

Have you concluded that, despite your best efforts, you have no system to mark your Book of Mormon? Or have you marked everything important to you in one color, only to find that it does not mean much since so much is marked—and everything is marked in the same way?

I answered yes to all of the above questions, and for this reason I developed and wrote *Make Your Mark in the Scriptures -In- the Book of Mormon.*

If you answered yes to some, or all, of the above questions, I think you will really like *Make Your Mark in the Scriptures -In- the Book of Mormon.*

Chapter One
Making Connections

I have found that gospel scholarship is all about reading and making connections between related scriptures. Once you start making these connections, scripture reading and study becomes compelling. *Make Your Mark in the Scriptures -In- the Book of Mormon* helps you make these connections by categorizing related scriptures by color so that they can be read side by side, one after another. This consecutive style of reading lets you acquire greater depth of gospel subjects and see a larger picture of the teachings and principles. Now you can master these scriptures with greater acceleration, accuracy, and breadth.

Make Your Mark in the Scriptures -In- the Book of Mormon also teaches you how to approach these scriptures, comprehend them in a meaningful way, and note them in a way that is useful to you. It becomes an easy and effective handbook to master, and then to teach, the great truths taught in the Book of Mormon—an important accomplishment since the Lord tells us we will be judged out of the scriptures.[2]

Make Your Mark in the Scriptures -In- the Book of Mormon becomes a compelling doctrinal approach to the Book of Mormon with corresponding color markings of its teachings and principles so they are ever present for study, review, or teaching.

Make Your Mark in the Scriptures -In- the Book of Mormon enables gospel readers to become gospel students, and gospel students to become gospel scholars, in a matter of months rather than in a matter of years.

It is, after all, just as President Boyd K. Packer has explained: "Individual doctrines are not fully explained in one place in the scriptures, nor presented in order of sequence. They must be assembled from pieces here and there. They are sometimes found in large segments, but mostly they are in small bits scattered throughout the chapters and verses. . . . Because the scriptures are arranged the way they are, there are endless combinations of truths that will fit the need of every individual in every circumstance."[3]

With *Make Your Mark in the Scriptures -In- the Book of Mormon* your confidence with the scriptures will soar, and your ability to learn and teach will likewise take flight.

You will be filled with the Spirit as you read and study the scriptures.[4] You will be blessed by the Lord because you will have sought him diligently.[5]

Fathers and mothers, you will be able to open the Book of Mormon and, with confidence, teach specific truths to your children.

Young men and young women, you can immerse yourselves in the Book of Mormon earlier and more often and feel that your time has really been productive.

Boys and girls, you will absolutely delight in colorfully marking your Book of Mormon and having your marks so meaningful, accurate, and enduring. And you will learn from this great book at your early age.

Church leaders, you will have another tool to help move members to new spiritual heights.

Missionaries, you will be better able to teach from the scriptures, allowing the Spirit to testify of truth.

And finally, you will now be able to go to the heart of the Book of Mormon for doctrine. You will be able to rely more on your own scholarship and less on commentary material. Such independence will produce great benefit, for the Spirit is most abundant in the scriptures.

Read each of the following brief chapters–chapters two through twelve–before you commence marking verses as instructed in chapters four through eleven.

Chapter Two
A Doctrinal Approach

This is a doctrinal approach to the Book of Mormon.

The order of marking is important.

This is how you start to mark:

- Mark the atonement scriptures (listed in chapter four) in red.

- Mark the keys to the atonement scriptures—faith, repentance, baptism, the Holy Ghost, and enduring well to the end (listed in chapter five)—in yellow.

- Mark the doctrines of the kingdom scriptures (listed in chapter six) in green.

- Mark the characteristics of Christ scriptures (listed in chapter seven) in orange.

- Mark the gospel principles and practices scriptures (listed in chapter eight) in blue.

- Mark the prophecy scriptures (listed in chapter nine) in purple.

- Mark the sophistries and strategies of the adversary scriptures and other negative concepts (listed in chapter ten) in black.

- Mark the informational scriptures (listed in chapter eleven) in brown.

A Doctrinal Approach

This is how you start to read and study:

I suggest that you read the colored verses in the order listed above: red, yellow, green, orange, blue, purple, black, and brown. Hence, read all the reds first, then all the yellows, then all the greens, etc. This order allows you to read the most important verses first and to continue reading in order of proposed importance and priority.

The verses marked in red, yellow, green, orange, blue, and purple will be infinitely more rich than those marked in black and brown. And the verses have prominence in about that same order as listed—the reds, yellows, greens, and oranges tend to teach, outright, more doctrine than the blues and purples, which teach more than the blacks and browns. Note as well, a verse that has several colors marked on it signifies greater abundance within that verse than a verse that perhaps has only one color marked on it.

Once you have marked your Book of Mormon as outlined in this book, your book will be set for life. You can thumb through the pages of your Book of Mormon and instantly identify the type of scriptures you are looking for. You can quickly note the prominent and richly laden substantive verses from the lesser important verses. As you read and study you will start to learn and comprehend in a totally new way.

If your current Book of Mormon is unmarked, or little marked, you can start right away. If your current Book of Mormon is marked, but marked without a meaningful and useful system, you may want to obtain a new copy of the Book of Mormon and then start. Your Book of Mormon marked as suggested above will become a key to a treasure within a treasure.

Remember that the marking takes a little time, but it is well worth it.

The marking colors comprise eight in all. You can buy eight colored pencils or one of those pencils that has eight rotating colors in it.

I mark the first color on each verse in the space for the number. Every color after the first color of each verse receives an area of space three letters long. I mark the colors quite darkly so they do not fade over time.

For a color example of how to mark your scriptures see the pictures on front and back covers of this book.

Chapter Three
Take Faith as an Example

May I show you how connections between related scriptures can and ought to be made?

Take faith as an example. As you read faith scriptures side by side you begin to see that faith has many components. In other words, to have greater faith, or more powerful faith, you need to develop the additional components or qualities.

King Benjamin established the foundation of faith to be faith in Christ. ("They were filled with joy, . . . because of the exceeding faith which they had in Jesus Christ who should come."[6])

Mormon, through his son Moroni, teaches the first component of faith to be adhering to the words of God and angels. ("Wherefore, by the ministering of angels, and by every word which proceeded forth out of the mouth of God, men began to exercise faith in Christ."[7])

Moroni teaches the second component of faith to be hope. ("How is it that ye can attain unto faith, save ye shall have hope?"[8])

Alma teaches the third component of faith to be hope in true, though unseen, things. ("Faith is not to have a perfect knowledge of things; therefore if ye have faith ye hope for things which are not seen, which are true."[9])

Moroni teaches the fourth component of faith to be that a witness of the truth comes after a trial of faith. ("Dispute not because ye see not, for ye receive no witness until after the trial of your faith."[10])

Moroni teaches the fifth component of faith to be a meek and lowly heart. ("I say unto you that he cannot have faith and hope, save he shall be meek, and lowly of heart."[11])

Moroni teaches the sixth component of faith to be in having the power of the Holy Ghost in our lives, and the seventh component of faith to be in having charity. ("If so, his faith and hope is vain, for none is acceptable before God, save the meek and lowly in heart; and if a man be meek and lowly in heart, and confess by the power of the Holy Ghost that Jesus is the Christ, he must needs have charity; for if he have not charity he is nothing; wherefore he must needs have charity."[12])

Moroni teaches the eighth component of faith to be a cleaving to all things good. ("They who have faith in him will cleave unto every good thing."[13]) Moroni notes that all good comes from Christ. (". . . all things which are good cometh of Christ."[14])

Joseph Smith taught the ninth component of faith to be mental exertion. ("When a man works by faith he works by mental exertion instead of physical force."[15]) Isaiah also notes the power of thought. ("The Lord of Hosts hath sworn, saying: surely as I have thought, so shall it come to pass; and as I have purposed, so shall it stand."[16]) And Paul underscores the power of faith and the word of God. ("Through faith we understand that the worlds were framed by the word of God."[17])

Mormon taught the tenth component of faith to be doubting nothing. ("Whoso believeth in Christ, doubting nothing, whatsoever he shall ask the Father in the name of Christ it shall be granted him."[18]) James, likewise, notes the importance of believing and asking without doubting in order to receive. ("But let him ask in faith, nothing waivering. For he that waivereth is like a wave of the sea driven with the wind and tossed. For let not that man think that he shall receive any thing of the Lord."[19])

In summary, the components of faith in Jesus Christ are as follows:

1. Adhering to the words of Gods and angels.
2. Having hope.
3. Having hope in true, though unseen, things.
4. Realizing that the witness of truth comes after a trial of faith.
5. Having a meek and lowly heart.
6. Having the power of the Holy Ghost.
7. Having charity.
8. Cleaving to all good things.
9. Working by mental exertion.
10. Doubting nothing.

In analysis, faith requires:

1. Believing and trusting in Christ.
2. Developing qualities like Christ.
3. Thinking like Christ.

In other words, having faith in Christ means becoming like Christ.

Do you see how reading and making connections between related scriptures works?

Do not worry about an inability to make connections between related verses at first. As you read, the connections will just seem to occur to you. And as you study the scriptures this way, you may find that the connections seem almost endless. The Holy Ghost will help you when you diligently study the Book of Mormon.

Chapter Four
The Atonement Scriptures

Jesus Christ's atonement pays the debt for our sins, cleanses us, soothes our suffering, covers our sorrows, and perfects us over time as we apply it in our lives. It also raises us from the dead and unites our spirits with our perfected bodies. The following scriptures teach the atonement of Jesus Christ.

The Atonement Scriptures
(Marked in Red)

1 Nephi 1: 14, 19
1 Nephi 6: 4
1 Nephi 10: 4, 5, 6, 9, 10, 11, 14, 17
1 Nephi 11: 27, 31, 32, 33
1 Nephi 12: 10, 11, 18
1 Nephi 13: 37, 40
1 Nephi 15: 14
1 Nephi 19: 10, 23
1 Nephi 21: 7, 16, 25, 26
1 Nephi 22: 12, 28, 31

2 Nephi 1: 10, 15
2 Nephi 2: 3, 4, 5, 6, 7, 8, 9, 10, 26, 27, 28
2 Nephi 6: 9, 11, 12, 14, 18
2 Nephi 9: 5, 6, 7, 8, 10, 11, 12, 13, 19, 21, 22, 23, 25, 26
2 Nephi 10: 2, 3, 24, 25
2 Nephi 11: 2, 6

2 Nephi 16: 7
2 Nephi 25: 13, 14, 16, 17, 18, 19, 20, 23, 26, 29
2 Nephi 26: 1, 3, 9, 12, 24, 27
2 Nephi 31: 4, 15, 16, 17, 18, 19, 20, 21
2 Nephi 33: 4, 6, 9

Jacob 4: 5, 11, 12
Jacob 6: 4, 8, 9, 11
Jacob 7: 12, 25

Enos 1: 5

Jarom 1: 11

Omni 1: 26

Words of Mormon 1: 8

Mosiah 3: 7, 8, 9, 10, 11, 12, 13, 15, 16, 17, 18, 19, 20, 26
Mosiah 4: 2, 3, 6, 7, 8, 10, 11, 12
Mosiah 5: 7, 8, 15
Mosiah 13: 28, 32, 33, 34, 35
Mosiah 14: 4, 5, 6, 7, 8, 9, 10, 11, 12
Mosiah 15: 1, 2, 3, 4, 5, 6, 7, 8, 9, 10, 11, 12, 14, 18, 19, 20, 21, 22, 23, 24, 25, 26, 27, 28, 31
Mosiah 16: 1, 2, 4, 5, 6, 7, 8, 9, 11, 13, 15
Mosiah 18: 2, 7, 9, 13, 20, 30
Mosiah 26: 22, 23, 24, 26, 29, 30
Mosiah 27: 24, 25, 26, 29, 36
Mosiah 28: 7

Alma 4: 14
Alma 5: 13, 15, 21, 27, 48
Alma 6: 8
Alma 7: 7, 11, 12, 13, 14, 25
Alma 9: 27, 28
Alma 11: 37, 39, 40, 41, 42, 43, 44, 45
Alma 12: 8, 12, 15, 18, 20, 22, 24, 25, 26, 30, 32, 33, 34
Alma 13: 2, 5, 11, 12, 16
Alma 15: 6, 8
Alma 16: 19

Alma 17: 16
Alma 18: 39
Alma 19: 13, 29
Alma 21: 7, 9
Alma 22: 6, 13, 14, 18
Alma 24: 10, 11, 12, 13, 15, 16
Alma 25: 16
Alma 26: 35, 36
Alma 27: 28
Alma 28: 8
Alma 29: 2
Alma 32: 13
Alma 33: 11, 22
Alma 34: 6, 7, 8, 9, 10, 11, 12, 13, 14, 15, 16, 17, 18, 31, 36, 37
Alma 36: 17, 18, 19, 20
Alma 37: 7, 8, 9
Alma 38: 8, 9
Alma 39: 15
Alma 40: 2, 3, 4, 5, 6, 7, 8, 9, 10, 11, 12, 14, 15, 16, 17, 18, 19, 20, 21, 22, 23, 24, 25
Alma 41: 2, 4, 5, 7, 8, 10, 13
Alma 42: 9, 11, 12, 13, 14, 15, 22, 23, 24, 25, 26, 30, 31
Alma 46: 39
Alma 58: 41

Helaman 5: 9, 10, 11, 12
Helaman 8: 15, 18, 23

12

Helaman 12: 22, 23
Helaman 13: 6
Helaman 14: 2, 13, 15, 16, 17, 20, 25, 29
Helaman 15: 13

3 Nephi 5: 20, 26
3 Nephi 6: 20
3 Nephi 9: 14, 15, 17, 19, 20, 21, 22
3 Nephi 10: 10
3 Nephi 11: 7, 10, 11, 14, 15, 33
3 Nephi 12: 19, 20
3 Nephi 15: 9
3 Nephi 16: 4
3 Nephi 18: 3, 7, 8, 11, 28, 29, 30, 32
3 Nephi 20: 3, 5, 8, 13
3 Nephi 22: 5, 8
3 Nephi 23: 5
3 Nephi 25: 2
3 Nephi 26: 5
3 Nephi 27: 6, 13, 14, 15, 16, 19, 20
3 Nephi 28: 10

Mormon 3: 21
Mormon 5: 14
Mormon 7: 3, 5, 6, 7
Mormon 9: 6, 11, 12, 13, 14, 23, 29

Ether 2: 15
Ether 3: 13, 14, 19, 20
Ether 4: 15, 18, 19
Ether 5: 5
Ether 12: 7, 8, 9, 11, 33, 37
Ether 13: 10, 11

Moroni 4: 3
Moroni 5: 2
Moroni 6: 2, 4, 6
Moroni 7: 27, 28, 34, 38, 41
Moroni 8: 8, 10, 11, 12, 17, 19, 20, 22
Moroni 9: 22, 25
Moroni 10: 32, 33

Chapter Five
The Keys to the Atonement Scriptures

The Atonement of Jesus Christ has two parts: a free gift and an earned gift. The free gift is the resurrection—we will live in our perfected bodies never to die again. The earned gift is eternal life—the life that God lives or eternal family life. The earned gift of eternal life is obtained by five keys to the atonement of Jesus Christ consistently applied in our lives. These keys are:

One   -   Faith in the Lord Jesus Christ ("Faith").
Two   -   Repentance ("Repentance").
Three -   Baptism by immersion for the remission of sins ("Baptism").
Four   -   The laying on of hands for the gift of the Holy Ghost ("Holy Ghost").
Five   -   Enduring well to the end ("Enduring").

The following scriptures teach the five keys to the Atonement of Jesus Christ: faith, repentance, baptism, the Holy Ghost, and enduring.

The Keys to the Atonement Scriptures:
Faith, Repentance, Baptism,
the Holy Ghost, and Enduring
(Marked in Yellow)

1 Nephi 1: 4, 7, 8, 12, 20
1 Nephi 2: 14, 17, 19
1 Nephi 3: 20
1 Nephi 4: 1, 6, 10, 11, 12, 13, 18
1 Nephi 5: 17

1 Nephi 7: 12, 13, 15, 17, 20, 21
1 Nephi 10: 9, 10, 11, 17, 18, 19, 22
1 Nephi 11: 1, 2, 4, 6, 8, 9, 11, 27
1 Nephi 12: 7, 10, 11, 18

1 Nephi 13: 37
1 Nephi 14: 5
1 Nephi 15: 11
1 Nephi 16: 25, 26, 28, 29, 39
1 Nephi 17: 7, 52
1 Nephi 18: 15, 20
1 Nephi 19: 23
1 Nephi 22: 2, 28, 31

2 Nephi 1: 6, 10, 27
2 Nephi 2: 4, 9, 21, 28
2 Nephi 3: 20, 21, 24
2 Nephi 4: 12
2 Nephi 5: 22
2 Nephi 6: 12, 14
2 Nephi 9: 18, 23, 24
2 Nephi 10: 7
2 Nephi 24: 24
2 Nephi 25: 4, 13, 16, 23, 24, 25, 28, 29
2 Nephi 26: 11, 13, 27
2 Nephi 27: 23
2 Nephi 28: 1, 4, 17, 19, 26, 31, 32
2 Nephi 30: 2
2 Nephi 31: 4, 5, 6, 8, 9, 10, 11, 12, 13, 14, 15, 16, 17, 18, 19, 20, 21
2 Nephi 32: 2, 3, 5, 7, 8
2 Nephi 33: 1, 2, 3, 4, 7, 9, 10

Jacob 1: 5, 8
Jacob 3: 1, 3, 4, 8
Jacob 4: 6, 11, 13, 15
Jacob 6: 5, 8, 11
Jacob 7: 5, 8, 12, 17

Enos 1: 2, 8, 10, 11, 12, 15, 16, 18

Jarom 1: 4, 12

Omni 1: 13, 20, 26

Words of Mormon 1: 7

Mosiah 2: 36, 38, 41
Mosiah 3: 9, 12, 13, 19, 21
Mosiah 4: 2, 3, 6, 9, 10, 11, 12, 18, 20, 21, 26, 30
Mosiah 5: 2, 3, 4, 5, 6, 7, 8, 9
Mosiah 6: 2
Mosiah 8: 18
Mosiah 10: 13
Mosiah 11: 20, 21, 23, 25
Mosiah 12: 8, 12
Mosiah 13: 5
Mosiah 15: 11
Mosiah 16: 12, 13
Mosiah 18: 1, 7, 8, 9, 10, 12, 13, 14, 15, 16, 17, 20, 21, 26
Mosiah 21: 30, 33, 34, 35

Mosiah 24: 16
Mosiah 25: 15, 17, 18, 22, 23, 24
Mosiah 26: 11, 14, 15, 16, 21, 22, 23, 29, 30, 31, 32, 35, 36, 37
Mosiah 27: 14, 24, 28, 35
Mosiah 28: 4
Mosiah 29: 19

Alma 2: 30
Alma 3: 14
Alma 4: 4, 5, 13, 14, 15, 20
Alma 5: 3, 12, 13, 14, 15, 31, 32, 33, 46, 47, 49, 50, 51, 54, 56, 62
Alma 6: 2, 3, 8
Alma 7: 5, 6, 8, 9, 10, 13, 14, 15, 16, 17, 24, 26, 27
Alma 8: 10, 15, 16, 24, 29, 30, 32
Alma 9: 12, 15, 18, 20, 21, 25, 27, 30
Alma 10: 12, 20, 23
Alma 11: 40
Alma 12: 3, 7, 15, 24, 30, 33, 34, 37
Alma 13: 3, 4, 10, 12, 13, 16, 18, 21, 26, 27, 28, 29, 30
Alma 14: 1, 6, 11, 26, 28
Alma 15: 6, 7, 8, 9, 10, 12, 13, 14

Alma 16: 13, 16
Alma 17: 3, 4, 9, 10, 15, 16
Alma 18: 16, 29, 33, 34, 35
Alma 19: 10, 13, 14, 23, 35, 36
Alma 20: 2, 17
Alma 21: 7, 16
Alma 22: 1, 4, 5, 6, 7, 11, 13, 14, 15, 16, 18
Alma 23: 6, 15
Alma 24: 8, 9, 10, 11, 12, 24
Alma 25: 16
Alma 26: 21, 22, 35
Alma 27: 8, 18, 23, 27
Alma 29: 1, 2, 9, 10
Alma 30: 57
Alma 31: 36, 38
Alma 32: 7, 13, 15, 16, 17, 18, 21, 22, 26, 27, 28, 29, 30, 31, 32, 33, 34, 35, 36, 37, 40, 41, 42, 43
Alma 33: 22, 23
Alma 34: 3, 4, 15, 16, 17, 30, 31, 33, 34, 35, 38
Alma 35: 14
Alma 36: 12, 13, 14, 15, 16, 17, 18, 19, 20, 21, 23, 24, 26
Alma 37: 9, 15, 22, 25, 26, 31, 33, 40, 41
Alma 38: 2, 6, 8
Alma 39: 6, 8, 9, 12, 13
Alma 41: 6

Alma 42: 4, 5, 13, 16, 17, 18, 22, 23, 24, 28, 29, 30, 31
Alma 43: 2
Alma 44: 3, 4, 5
Alma 46: 39, 41
Alma 48: 19
Alma 49: 30
Alma 54: 6, 7
Alma 57: 21, 26, 27
Alma 58: 11, 40
Alma 60: 26
Alma 61: 17, 20
Alma 62: 45

Helaman 3: 24, 26, 28, 35
Helaman 4: 14, 15, 16, 24
Helaman 5: 11, 17, 19, 29, 30, 31, 32, 33, 41, 44, 45, 46, 47
Helaman 6: 1, 4, 35, 36
Helaman 7: 17, 19, 22, 23, 24, 28
Helaman 8: 15, 26
Helaman 9: 22
Helaman 10: 11, 12, 14, 16, 17
Helaman 11: 4, 9, 14, 15
Helaman 12: 22, 23, 24
Helaman 13: 2, 3, 4, 5, 6, 8, 10, 11, 13, 36, 38, 39
Helaman 14: 2, 8, 9, 11, 12, 13, 18, 19, 29
Helaman 15: 1, 2, 3, 7, 9, 14, 17

Helaman 16: 1, 3, 4, 5

3 Nephi 1: 12, 23
3 Nephi 3: 15, 25
3 Nephi 4: 33
3 Nephi 5: 3, 4
3 Nephi 7: 16, 18, 21, 22, 23, 24, 25, 26
3 Nephi 9: 1, 2, 13, 17, 20, 22
3 Nephi 10: 3, 6
3 Nephi 11: 3, 4, 5, 6, 21, 22, 23, 24, 25, 26, 27, 28, 32, 33, 35, 36, 37, 38
3 Nephi 12: 1, 2, 6, 19
3 Nephi 13: 11, 14, 15
3 Nephi 15: 9, 23
3 Nephi 16: 4, 6, 13
3 Nephi 17: 8, 20
3 Nephi 18: 5, 7, 10, 11, 16, 20, 30, 31, 32, 37
3 Nephi 19: 9, 10, 11, 12, 13, 20, 21, 22, 23, 28, 29, 35
3 Nephi 20: 9, 15, 20, 27, 31
3 Nephi 21: 2, 6, 14, 20, 22
3 Nephi 23: 5
3 Nephi 26: 9, 11, 17, 21
3 Nephi 27: 1, 5, 6, 16, 19, 20, 33
3 Nephi 28: 11, 18
3 Nephi 29: 6
3 Nephi 30: 2

4 Nephi 1: 1, 48

Mormon 1: 14
Mormon 2: 10, 13, 14
Mormon 3: 2, 3, 15, 16, 20, 21, 22
Mormon 5: 11, 22, 24
Mormon 6: 22
Mormon 7: 3, 5, 8, 10
Mormon 8: 24
Mormon 9: 21, 23, 24, 25, 27, 29, 37

Ether 2: 11, 15
Ether 3: 4, 5, 6, 7, 8, 9, 10, 11, 12, 14, 15, 19, 26
Ether 4: 6, 7, 11, 18, 19
Ether 5: 4, 5
Ether 7: 13, 23, 25, 26
Ether 8: 23
Ether 9: 28, 34
Ether 11: 1, 6, 8, 12, 20
Ether 12: 2, 3, 4, 6, 7, 8, 9, 10, 11, 12, 13, 14, 15, 16, 17, 18, 19, 20, 21, 22, 23, 27, 28, 29, 30, 31, 37, 41
Ether 13: 20
Ether 15: 3

Moroni 2: 2, 3
Moroni 3: 3, 4

Moroni 4: 3
Moroni 5: 2
Moroni 6: 1, 2, 3, 4, 8, 9
Moroni 7: 25, 26, 28, 30, 31, 32, 33, 34, 36, 37, 38, 39, 40, 41, 42, 43, 44
Moroni 8: 3, 7, 8, 9, 10, 11, 16, 19, 22, 23, 24, 25, 26, 28
Moroni 9: 22, 25
Moroni 10: 4, 5, 7, 8, 9, 10, 11, 12, 13, 14, 15, 16, 17, 18, 20, 21, 23, 24, 30, 33

Chapter Six
The Doctrines of the Kingdom Scriptures

Prophets through the ages have revealed, and recorded in holy writ, the doctrines of the kingdom. These doctrines help us with the process of working out our salvation through Christ and instruct us in the perfecting process through the Holy Ghost. This chapter contains the doctrinal scriptures (excepting those already noted atonement and keys to the atonement scriptures listed in chapters four and five) and are classic scriptures that are worth reviewing often. The following scriptures teach the doctrines of the kingdom.

The Doctrines of the Kingdom Scriptures
(Marked in Green)

1 Nephi 1: 5, 6, 8, 9, 10, 11, 12, 14

1 Nephi 2: 20

1 Nephi 3: 7, 20

1 Nephi 4: 1, 6, 14

1 Nephi 5: 17

1 Nephi 6: 4

1 Nephi 7: 1, 12

1 Nephi 8: 2, 10, 11, 12, 15, 19, 20, 24

1 Nephi 9: 6

1 Nephi 10: 12, 13, 14, 17, 18, 19, 20, 21, 22

1 Nephi 11: 6, 11, 16, 17, 21, 22, 23, 25, 26, 27, 28, 30, 31

1 Nephi 12: 7, 9, 18

1 Nephi 13: 23, 24, 34, 37, 39, 40, 41, 42

1 Nephi 14: 7

1 Nephi 15: 14, 18, 25, 32, 33, 34, 35, 36

1 Nephi 17: 3, 13, 15, 35, 39, 40, 55

1 Nephi 18: 3

1 Nephi 19: 15, 16, 17

1 Nephi 22: 2, 8, 9, 10, 11, 15, 16, 17, 19, 20, 21, 24, 25, 26, 28, 30, 31

2 Nephi 1: 15, 16, 19, 20, 26, 27

2 Nephi 2: 3, 4, 5, 6, 7, 8, 9, 10, 11, 12, 13, 14, 15, 16, 20, 21, 24, 25, 26, 27, 28

2 Nephi 3: 7, 12

2 Nephi 4: 34, 35
2 Nephi 6: 12
2 Nephi 8: 13
2 Nephi 9: 5, 6, 7, 8, 10, 11, 12, 13, 14, 15, 16, 17, 18, 19, 20, 21, 22, 23, 24, 25, 26, 27, 38, 39, 40, 41, 43, 44, 45, 46, 48, 49, 51, 52, 53
2 Nephi 10: 7, 8, 23, 24, 25
2 Nephi 11: 2, 3, 5, 7
2 Nephi 25: 16, 17, 18, 22, 23, 25, 26, 27, 28, 29, 30
2 Nephi 26: 1, 7, 8, 12, 24, 33
2 Nephi 27: 23
2 Nephi 28: 23, 32
2 Nephi 29: 1, 2, 7, 9, 11, 14
2 Nephi 30: 1, 2
2 Nephi 31: 6, 7, 9, 10, 11, 12, 13, 14, 15, 16, 17, 18, 19, 20, 21
2 Nephi 32: 3, 6, 8, 9
2 Nephi 33: 4, 9, 10, 11, 12, 14, 15

Jacob 1: 6, 7, 8, 17, 19
Jacob 2: 2, 4, 5, 17, 18, 19, 21, 27, 28, 29
Jacob 3: 1, 2, 7
Jacob 4: 4, 5, 6, 7, 8, 9, 10, 13
Jacob 5: 4, 7, 8, 11, 13, 18, 20, 23, 24, 47, 54, 60, 72, 74, 75, 76

Jacob 6: 4, 5, 8, 9, 10, 11
Jacob 7: 5, 11, 14, 17, 19, 22, 23, 25

Enos 1: 5, 10, 27

Jarom 1: 4, 5, 11

Omni 1: 13, 25, 26

Words of Mormon 1: 7, 11

Mosiah 1: 2, 7, 11, 16
Mosiah 2: 4, 9, 11, 15, 16, 17, 19, 20, 21, 22, 23, 24, 25, 26, 27, 28, 31, 33, 34, 35, 36, 37, 38, 39, 40, 41
Mosiah 3: 2, 4, 5, 6, 8, 10, 11, 13, 16, 17, 18, 19, 21, 24, 26
Mosiah 4: 2, 3, 6, 7, 8, 9, 10, 11, 12, 14, 15, 16, 18, 19, 20, 21, 22, 26, 27, 30
Mosiah 5: 2, 3, 5, 7, 8, 9, 10, 11, 12, 13, 15
Mosiah 6: 6
Mosiah 7: 19, 27, 33
Mosiah 8: 16, 17, 18
Mosiah 12: 29, 33, 35, 36
Mosiah 13: 12, 13, 14, 15, 16, 17, 18, 19, 20, 21, 22, 23, 24, 33, 34

Mosiah 15: 2, 3, 4, 5, 6, 7, 8, 9, 10, 11, 12, 13, 14, 22, 23, 24, 25, 26, 27, 28, 29, 30, 31

Mosiah 16: 1, 2, 4, 5, 6, 9, 10, 11, 12, 14, 15

Mosiah 18: 8, 9, 10, 13, 16, 17, 23, 25, 26, 27, 28, 29

Mosiah 21: 31, 32, 35

Mosiah 23: 7, 14, 15, 18, 21, 22, 23

Mosiah 24: 21, 22

Mosiah 26: 20, 21, 22, 23, 24, 25, 27, 28, 29, 30, 31, 32, 33, 35, 36, 38, 39

Mosiah 27: 14, 25, 26, 27, 28, 29, 30, 31, 37

Mosiah 29: 20

Alma 1: 25, 27, 30

Alma 3: 26, 27

Alma 4: 13, 14, 19, 20

Alma 5: 3, 7, 9, 12, 13, 14, 15, 16, 18, 19, 21, 24, 25, 26, 27, 28, 29, 34, 35, 38, 40, 41, 44, 46, 47, 48, 49, 50

Alma 6: 6, 8

Alma 7: 6, 8, 13, 14, 15, 16, 19, 20, 21, 23, 24, 25, 26, 27

Alma 8: 15, 24

Alma 9: 13, 20, 21, 26, 28

Alma 10: 7, 12

Alma 11: 37, 39, 40, 41, 43, 44, 45

Alma 12: 3, 7, 8, 9, 10, 12, 14, 15, 16, 20, 21, 22, 23, 24, 25, 26, 27, 28, 29, 30, 31, 32, 33, 34, 36, 37

Alma 13: 1, 2, 3, 4, 5, 6, 7, 8, 9, 10, 11, 12, 15, 16, 18, 22, 26, 28, 29

Alma 15: 17

Alma 16: 5

Alma 17: 2, 3, 9

Alma 18: 28, 32, 34, 35, 36, 39

Alma 19: 6, 14

Alma 21: 9, 16, 23

Alma 22: 10, 12, 13, 14, 15, 16, 18

Alma 23: 6

Alma 24: 14, 15, 18

Alma 25: 16

Alma 26: 8, 22, 35, 37

Alma 28: 12

Alma 29: 4, 5, 11, 13, 17

Alma 30: 3

Alma 31: 10

Alma 32: 13, 15, 20, 23, 35, 42

Alma 33: 11, 22, 23

Alma 34: 2, 15, 16, 17, 18, 19, 20, 21, 22, 23, 24, 25, 26, 27, 28, 29, 36, 37, 38

Alma 36: 1, 2, 3, 4, 5, 15, 27, 28, 30

Alma 37: 12, 13, 15, 16, 20, 35, 36, 37, 44, 45

Alma 38: 1, 5, 6, 9, 14, 15

Alma 39: 6, 14

Alma 40: 11, 12, 21, 22, 24, 25, 26

Alma 41: 2, 3, 4, 5, 6, 7, 8, 10, 11, 12, 13, 14, 15

Alma 42: 1, 2, 3, 4, 5, 6, 7, 8, 9, 10, 11, 12, 13, 14, 15, 16, 17, 18, 22, 23, 24, 25, 26, 27, 30, 31

Alma 43: 2, 10

Alma 45: 1, 16

Alma 48: 15, 16, 19, 20, 25

Alma 49: 28, 30

Alma 50: 19, 20, 22

Alma 53: 10, 21

Alma 58: 10, 11, 40, 41

Alma 60: 23

Alma 62: 51

Alma 63: 2

Helaman 3: 27, 28, 29, 30, 35

Helaman 4: 23, 24, 25

Helaman 5: 4, 6, 8, 9, 11, 12, 14, 17, 18, 23, 45, 47, 48

Helaman 7: 2

Helaman 8: 18, 23

Helaman 10: 3, 4, 5, 6, 7, 16, 17

Helaman 11: 3

Helaman 12: 24, 25, 26

Helaman 13: 1, 3, 4, 7, 8, 38

Helaman 14: 8, 12, 15, 16, 17, 18, 19, 29, 30, 31

Helaman 15: 7

3 Nephi 1: 13, 14

3 Nephi 3: 19

3 Nephi 4: 30

3 Nephi 5: 13, 24, 25, 26

3 Nephi 6: 14

3 Nephi 7: 15, 18, 19, 20, 21

3 Nephi 8: 1

3 Nephi 9: 14, 15, 17, 18, 22

3 Nephi 10: 10

3 Nephi 11: 7, 10, 11, 12, 14, 21, 22, 25, 27, 32, 33, 35, 36, 38, 39, 40

3 Nephi 12: 1, 16, 18, 19, 20, 21, 22, 27, 28, 43, 44, 45, 48

3 Nephi 13: 6, 8, 9, 10, 11, 12, 13, 14, 15, 22, 33

3 Nephi 14: 1, 2, 7, 8, 11, 12, 14, 21

3 Nephi 15: 1, 9, 10, 17, 21

3 Nephi 16: 3, 4, 5, 6

3 Nephi 17: 3, 9, 15, 24

3 Nephi 18: 15, 16, 18, 19, 20, 21, 23, 24, 37

3 Nephi 19: 6, 7, 8, 9, 14, 15, 16, 17, 18, 23, 25, 27, 28, 29, 30, 31, 35
3 Nephi 20: 1, 8, 9, 10, 22, 23, 25, 26, 27, 31, 35
3 Nephi 21: 6, 9, 11, 20
3 Nephi 23: 5, 9
3 Nephi 24: 2, 3, 5, 6, 7, 8, 10, 11, 12, 18
3 Nephi 25: 6
3 Nephi 26: 2, 4, 5, 14, 15, 17
3 Nephi 27: 1, 2, 6, 7, 13, 14, 15, 16, 17, 18, 19, 20, 21, 25, 26, 27, 28, 29, 33
3 Nephi 28: 1, 3, 6, 7, 8, 9, 10, 11, 12, 13, 15, 17, 29, 30, 31, 32, 34, 35, 36, 37, 38, 39, 40
3 Nephi 29: 1, 2, 6
3 Nephi 30: 1

4 Nephi 1: 3, 5, 11, 12, 15, 16, 17, 18, 30

Mormon 1: 15
Mormon 2: 14, 19
Mormon 3: 12, 20, 21
Mormon 5: 14, 17, 23
Mormon 6: 17, 21, 22
Mormon 7: 5, 6, 7, 8, 10
Mormon 8: 10, 15, 17, 19, 20, 21, 22, 23, 24, 26

Mormon 9: 2, 5, 6, 7, 9, 11, 12, 13, 14, 15, 16, 17, 18, 19, 20, 21, 22, 23, 24, 25, 27, 28, 29, 35, 36, 37

Ether 2: 12, 15
Ether 3: 2, 4, 6, 7, 8, 9, 12, 13, 14, 15, 16, 17, 19, 20, 25, 26
Ether 4: 7, 9, 12, 15, 18, 19
Ether 5: 4, 5
Ether 6: 17
Ether 8: 26
Ether 12: 2, 6, 8, 9, 10, 11, 21, 28, 32, 33, 34, 37, 38, 39, 41
Ether 13: 11
Ether 15: 34

Moroni 1: 2, 3
Moroni 2: 2, 3
Moroni 3: 2, 3, 4
Moroni 4: 2, 3
Moroni 5: 2
Moroni 6: 2, 3, 4, 5
Moroni 7: 2, 16, 22, 23, 24, 25, 26, 27, 28, 29, 30, 31, 32, 33, 36, 37, 38, 39, 40, 41, 42, 43, 44, 45, 46, 47, 48
Moroni 8: 3, 7, 8, 16, 17, 18, 21, 22, 24, 25, 26
Moroni 9: 25, 26

Moroni 10: 3, 4, 5, 6, 7, 8, 9, 10,
    11, 12, 13, 14, 15, 16, 17, 18,
    19, 20, 21, 23, 26, 27, 30, 31,
    32, 33, 34

Chapter Seven
The Characteristics of Christ Scriptures

    Jesus Christ commanded that we be perfect even as he is perfect. He declared it this way to the Nephites after his resurrection: "Therefore I would that ye should be perfect even as I, or your Father who is in heaven is perfect."[20] Christ wants us to attain the attributes he has. The following scriptures teach the characteristics of our Lord and Savior—which we can learn and develop through the tutelage of the Holy Ghost.

The Characteristics of Christ Scriptures
(Marked in Orange)

1 Nephi 1: 1, 14, 20
1 Nephi 2: 9, 10, 19
1 Nephi 5: 4
1 Nephi 8: 8
1 Nephi 9: 6
1 Nephi 11: 16, 17, 22, 23, 25, 26
1 Nephi 13: 29, 33, 34
1 Nephi 17: 42
1 Nephi 18: 4
1 Nephi 19: 9, 20
1 Nephi 20: 12, 14
1 Nephi 21: 10, 13
1 Nephi 22: 21

2 Nephi 1: 2, 3, 10, 19
2 Nephi 2: 3, 6, 7, 8, 10, 12, 24
2 Nephi 4: 7, 17, 21, 26, 32, 33

2 Nephi 6: 11
2 Nephi 8: 3, 5, 6, 15, 16, 22
2 Nephi 9: 8, 10, 17, 18, 19, 20, 21, 40, 41, 42, 44, 53
2 Nephi 10: 20, 24
2 Nephi 11: 5
2 Nephi 15: 16
2 Nephi 16: 3
2 Nephi 17: 15
2 Nephi 19: 17, 21
2 Nephi 21: 2, 3, 4, 5, 10
2 Nephi 23: 22
2 Nephi 24: 1, 24
2 Nephi 25: 13, 16
2 Nephi 26: 9, 30
2 Nephi 27: 22, 27
2 Nephi 28: 14, 32
2 Nephi 29: 9

2 Nephi 30: 9, 11
2 Nephi 31: 7, 13
2 Nephi 33: 7, 8, 9

Jacob 3: 6
Jacob 4: 7, 10
Jacob 5: 4, 5, 7, 8, 9, 11, 13, 15,
    20, 22, 23, 24, 25, 28, 32, 41,
    46, 47, 49, 51, 52, 54, 58, 60,
    61, 62, 63, 64, 66, 71, 72, 75
Jacob 6: 4, 5

Jarom 1: 3

Words of Mormon 1: 17

Mosiah 1: 13
Mosiah 2: 11
Mosiah 3: 5, 7, 8, 18, 19
Mosiah 4: 2, 5, 6, 9, 10, 11, 12
Mosiah 5: 2, 3, 15
Mosiah 8: 20
Mosiah 14: 2, 3, 4, 5, 6, 7, 9, 11,
    12
Mosiah 15: 5, 6, 7, 9, 14, 15, 16,
    17, 18, 30
Mosiah 16: 9, 12
Mosiah 18: 8, 9, 16
Mosiah 21: 13, 14
Mosiah 24: 13, 16, 21
Mosiah 25: 10

Mosiah 27: 28, 31, 37
Mosiah 28: 4
Mosiah 29: 19, 20

Alma 4: 13, 14
Alma 5: 4, 6, 9, 13, 14, 27, 33,
    48, 50
Alma 7: 2, 3, 4, 11, 12, 13, 23,
    24, 27
Alma 9: 7, 11, 16, 17, 26
Alma 10: 5
Alma 11: 39
Alma 12: 15, 32, 33
Alma 13: 7, 9, 13, 14, 28, 29
Alma 15: 17
Alma 17: 11, 31
Alma 18: 22, 41
Alma 19: 29, 34
Alma 24: 14, 15
Alma 26: 8, 11, 15, 16, 20, 27,
    28, 29, 35, 36, 37
Alma 27: 17, 18
Alma 28: 14
Alma 29: 8, 10
Alma 31: 38
Alma 32: 7, 8, 12, 13, 14, 15, 16,
    21, 22, 41, 42, 43
Alma 33: 4, 5, 8, 9, 11, 16, 23
Alma 34: 3, 15, 16, 17, 18, 19, 29,
    38, 39, 40, 41
Alma 36: 25, 29

Alma 37: 9, 12, 16, 20, 33, 34, 35, 47
Alma 38: 2, 3, 4, 5, 7, 8, 9, 10, 12, 14, 15
Alma 41: 14
Alma 42: 15, 24, 30, 31
Alma 46: 41
Alma 49: 28
Alma 50: 19
Alma 53: 21
Alma 57: 25, 26, 36
Alma 62: 41, 49

Helaman 3: 27
Helaman 4: 25
Helaman 5: 47
Helaman 6: 5
Helaman 7: 24
Helaman 8: 15, 17
Helaman 12: 1, 2, 6
Helaman 14: 12
Helaman 15: 12, 13

3 Nephi 1: 13
3 Nephi 4: 32, 33
3 Nephi 5: 21
3 Nephi 6: 13, 14
3 Nephi 9: 14, 15, 18, 22
3 Nephi 11: 11, 37, 38
3 Nephi 12: 2, 3, 4, 5, 6, 7, 8, 9, 10, 11, 12, 19, 48

3 Nephi 13: 8, 9
3 Nephi 15: 9
3 Nephi 16: 9
3 Nephi 17: 6, 7, 17, 20, 21, 22
3 Nephi 21: 10
3 Nephi 22: 7, 8, 10, 17
3 Nephi 24: 2, 3, 6
3 Nephi 25: 2
3 Nephi 26: 5
3 Nephi 27: 27, 30, 31
3 Nephi 28: 10

4 Nephi 1: 34

Mormon 2: 12
Mormon 3: 12
Mormon 5: 23
Mormon 6: 22
Mormon 8: 17
Mormon 9: 5, 9, 11, 18, 19

Ether 1: 35, 37, 40
Ether 3: 2, 3, 4, 12
Ether 4: 7, 12
Ether 6: 12, 17, 30
Ether 8: 26
Ether 9: 2, 22
Ether 11: 8
Ether 12: 26, 27, 28, 29, 32, 34, 36, 39, 41
Ether 13: 7

Moroni 7: 1, 2, 3, 4, 22, 39, 40,
    41, 42, 43, 44, 45, 46, 47, 48
Moroni 8: 3, 10, 16, 17, 18, 19,
    20, 21, 23, 26
Moroni 9: 25, 26
Moroni 10: 3, 4, 7, 19, 20, 21, 32,
    33

Chapter Eight
The Gospel Principles and Practices Scriptures

     In addition to the doctrines of the kingdom discussed in chapter six, the gospel of Jesus Christ teaches gospel principles and practices to help us have a happier life and be more effective in all of our relationships and dealings in life. These principles and practices are sometimes taught directly and sometimes taught indirectly, through inference, in the scriptures. The following scriptures teach these principles and practices.

The Gospel Principles and Practices Scriptures
(Marked in Blue)

1 Nephi 1: 1, 7, 15, 16, 18

1 Nephi 2: 1, 2, 3, 7, 9, 10, 12, 14, 15, 16, 17, 18, 19, 21, 22, 23, 24

1 Nephi 3: 2, 5, 6, 8, 15, 16, 19, 21, 29

1 Nephi 4: 2, 3, 15, 18, 31, 32, 33, 34, 37

1 Nephi 5: 4, 5, 6, 7, 8, 9, 10, 14, 20, 21, 22

1 Nephi 6: 5, 6

1 Nephi 7: 4, 5, 8, 9, 10, 11, 13, 14, 15, 17, 18, 19, 20, 21, 22

1 Nephi 8: 8, 17, 30, 37, 38

1 Nephi 9: 3, 5

1 Nephi 10: 2, 3, 6, 8

1 Nephi 11: 1, 2, 3, 4, 5, 7, 8, 9, 10, 19

1 Nephi 13: 16, 30

1 Nephi 14: 1, 2, 5, 8, 10, 12, 14, 17, 29, 30

1 Nephi 15: 3, 6, 8, 9, 10, 11, 12, 13, 15, 16, 20, 21, 22, 23, 24, 26, 28, 30, 31

1 Nephi 16: 1, 2, 3, 4, 5, 7, 8, 9, 10, 23, 24, 25, 26, 27, 29, 32, 39

1 Nephi 17: 2, 5, 7, 8, 9, 10, 11, 12, 14, 16, 17, 18, 23, 29, 30, 31, 32, 33, 34, 36, 37, 38, 41, 42, 44, 45, 46, 47, 48, 49, 50, 51, 52, 53, 54

1 Nephi 18: 1, 2, 4, 5, 6, 10, 11, 12, 15, 16, 17, 18, 19, 20, 21, 24

1 Nephi 19: 1, 2, 3, 4, 5, 6, 7, 9, 10, 11, 12, 18, 19, 22, 23, 24

1 Nephi 20: 1, 2, 3, 4, 5, 6, 7, 8, 9, 10, 11, 12, 13, 14, 15, 16, 17, 18, 19, 20, 21, 22

1 Nephi 21: 1, 2, 3, 4, 5, 6, 8, 9, 10, 13, 14, 15, 18, 22, 23, 25, 26

1 Nephi 22: 1, 3, 6, 18, 22

2 Nephi 1: 1, 3, 5, 6, 7, 8, 9, 10, 12, 13, 14, 21, 22, 23, 24, 25, 28, 29, 30, 31, 32

2 Nephi 2: 1, 2, 19, 22, 23, 30

2 Nephi 3: 1, 2, 3, 4, 21, 23, 24, 25

2 Nephi 4: 3, 4, 5, 12, 13, 15, 16, 17, 18, 19, 20, 21, 22, 23, 24, 25, 26, 27, 28, 29, 30, 31, 32, 33

2 Nephi 5: 1, 5, 6, 10, 11, 14, 15, 16, 17, 18, 19, 20, 25, 26, 27, 30, 31, 32

2 Nephi 6: 2, 3, 4, 5

2 Nephi 7: 1, 2, 3, 4, 5, 7, 8, 9, 10

2 Nephi 8: 1, 2, 4, 5, 6, 7, 8, 9, 10, 11, 12, 16, 17, 22, 24

2 Nephi 9: 1, 2, 3, 4, 29, 42, 47, 50

2 Nephi 10: 1, 4, 12, 13, 14, 15, 16, 17, 18, 19, 20, 21, 22

2 Nephi 11: 4

2 Nephi 12: 5, 6

2 Nephi 13: 9, 10, 11

2 Nephi 15: 2, 16

2 Nephi 16: 1, 8, 9, 10

2 Nephi 17: 3, 4, 10, 11, 12, 13, 15, 16

2 Nephi 18: 3, 5, 11, 12, 13, 14, 16, 17, 18, 19, 20

2 Nephi 19: 12, 17, 21

2 Nephi 20: 4

2 Nephi 21: 3

2 Nephi 22: 1, 2, 3, 4, 5, 6

2 Nephi 23: 2, 3

2 Nephi 24: 24, 27

2 Nephi 25: 3, 4, 5, 6, 7, 8, 20, 21, 24

2 Nephi 26: 11, 13, 15, 17, 23, 25, 26, 27, 28, 29, 30, 31, 32

2 Nephi 28: 2, 17, 28, 30

2 Nephi 29: 4, 5, 8, 10, 12

2 Nephi 30: 5, 6, 7, 8, 9, 10, 11, 15, 16, 17, 18

2 Nephi 31: 2, 3, 5

2 Nephi 32: 1, 2, 4, 5, 7

2 Nephi 33: 3, 5, 6, 8

Jacob 1: 2, 4, 10, 18

Jacob 2: 3, 6, 7, 8, 9, 10, 11, 13, 14, 15, 16, 20, 25, 26, 30, 31, 32, 33, 34, 35

Jacob 3: 5, 6, 9, 10, 11, 12

Jacob 4: 3, 14, 17, 18

Jacob 5: 2, 3, 5, 9, 10, 12, 14, 15, 16, 17, 19, 22, 25, 26, 27, 28, 29, 30, 31, 32, 33, 34, 35, 36, 37, 38, 39, 40, 41, 42, 43, 44, 45, 46, 48, 49, 50, 51, 52, 53, 57, 58, 59, 61, 62, 63, 64, 65, 66, 68, 69, 70, 71, 73, 77

Jacob 6: 3, 6, 7, 12, 13

Jacob 7: 8, 9, 10, 15, 21, 24, 26, 27

Enos 1: 1, 2, 3, 4, 6, 7, 8, 9, 11, 12, 13, 14, 17, 19, 20, 22, 23, 26

Jarom 1: 7, 9, 10, 12

Omni 1: 6, 7, 12, 22

Words of Mormon 1: 8, 9, 14, 15, 16, 17, 18

Mosiah 1: 3, 4, 5, 6, 12, 13, 17, 18

Mosiah 2: 1, 3, 8, 10, 12, 13, 14, 18, 30

Mosiah 3: 3, 14, 22, 23

Mosiah 4: 1, 4, 5, 13, 17, 23, 24, 25, 28, 29

Mosiah 5: 1, 6, 14

Mosiah 6: 1, 3, 7

Mosiah 7: 12, 13, 16, 18, 20, 21, 25, 26, 29, 30, 31, 32

Mosiah 8: 13, 14, 15, 19, 20

Mosiah 9: 3, 15, 17, 18

Mosiah 10: 2, 7, 10, 11, 13, 14, 16, 19, 22

Mosiah 11: 2, 20, 21, 22, 23, 24, 25

Mosiah 12: 1, 2, 3, 4, 5, 6, 7, 8, 19, 21, 22, 23, 24, 25, 26, 27, 30, 31, 34, 37

Mosiah 13: 2, 3, 4, 5, 6, 7, 8, 9, 10, 11, 25, 26, 27, 29, 30, 31

Mosiah 15: 16, 17, 18

Mosiah 17: 2, 4, 9, 10, 11, 15, 19, 20

Mosiah 18: 3, 11, 12, 18, 19, 21, 22, 24, 30

Mosiah 20: 11, 14, 17, 21, 22, 24, 26

Mosiah 21: 4, 6, 13, 14, 15, 17, 30, 33, 34

Mosiah 22: 1, 3, 4, 14

Mosiah 23: 1, 2, 5, 6, 8, 9, 10, 11, 13, 16, 17, 19, 24, 27, 28, 29, 34

Mosiah 24: 6, 10, 12, 13, 14, 15, 16, 17, 19, 23

Mosiah 25: 8, 9, 10, 11, 12, 15, 16, 17, 18, 19, 20, 21, 22, 23, 24

Mosiah 26: 6, 8, 10, 11, 12, 13, 14, 17, 18, 19, 34, 37

Mosiah 27: 3, 4, 5, 7, 11, 13, 15, 16, 17, 18, 20, 21, 22, 23, 32, 33, 35, 36

Mosiah 28: 1, 2, 3, 4, 5, 6, 7, 13, 14, 15, 16, 20

Mosiah 29: 5, 8, 10, 11, 12, 13, 14, 15, 16, 19, 24, 25, 26, 28, 29, 30, 31, 32, 33, 34, 37, 38, 39, 40, 41, 42, 43, 45

Alma 1: 1, 7, 8, 9, 10, 13, 14, 20, 21, 24, 26, 29, 31, 33

Alma 2: 3, 5, 6, 7, 12, 16, 18, 21, 28, 30, 31

Alma 3: 6, 7, 8, 9, 11, 12, 14, 15, 16, 17, 19, 24

Alma 4: 3, 4, 5, 6, 7, 10, 15, 16, 18

Alma 5: 1, 4, 5, 6, 10, 11, 17, 33, 43, 45, 51, 52, 54, 57, 58, 59, 60, 61, 62

Alma 6: 1, 5

Alma 7: 3, 5, 9, 22

Alma 8: 4, 8, 10, 14, 16, 17, 18, 19, 20, 21, 22, 23, 25, 26, 29, 30, 31, 32

Alma 9: 1, 5, 7, 8, 9, 10, 11, 12, 14, 15, 16, 17, 18, 19, 22, 23, 24, 25, 29, 30, 33

Alma 10: 5, 8, 9, 10, 11, 17, 19, 20, 21, 22, 23, 25, 26, 27

Alma 11: 22, 23, 27, 29, 31, 32, 33, 34, 36, 46

Alma 12: 1, 11, 13, 35

Alma 13: 13, 14, 19, 20, 23, 24, 25, 27

Alma 14: 1, 3, 7, 10, 11, 13, 17, 18, 23, 26, 27, 28, 29

Alma 15: 2, 3, 5, 6, 8, 10, 11, 12, 13, 16, 18

Alma 16: 6, 9, 10, 14, 15, 16, 17, 18, 21

Alma 17: 4, 5, 6, 8, 10, 11, 12, 13, 14, 15, 17, 18, 23, 25, 29, 30, 31, 35, 36

Alma 18: 3, 9, 10, 12, 14, 15, 16, 17, 18, 19, 20, 22, 23, 24, 25, 26, 27, 29, 30, 31, 33, 38, 40, 41

Alma 19: 4, 9, 12, 13, 15, 16, 17, 23, 24, 25, 27, 29, 30, 31, 32, 33, 34, 35, 36

Alma 20: 1, 2, 3, 4, 5, 7, 15, 17, 18, 21, 22, 24, 25, 26, 27, 28, 29

Alma 21: 11, 12, 14, 15, 17, 19, 20, 21, 22

Alma 22: 1, 3, 4, 7, 8, 9, 11, 17, 20, 22, 23, 25, 26

Alma 23: 1, 3, 4, 5, 7, 8, 15, 18

Alma 24: 5, 6, 7, 8, 9, 12, 16, 17, 19, 21, 22, 23, 24, 25, 26, 27, 29, 30

Alma 25: 6, 14, 15, 17

Alma 26: 1, 2, 3, 4, 5, 6, 7, 9, 10, 11, 12, 13, 14, 15, 16, 17, 20, 21, 23, 24, 26, 27, 28, 29, 30, 31, 32, 33, 34, 36

Alma 27: 4, 7, 8, 9, 10, 11, 12, 13, 15, 16, 17, 18, 19, 21, 22, 24, 27, 28, 30

Alma 28: 6, 8, 11, 13, 14

Alma 29: 1, 2, 3, 6, 7, 8, 9, 10, 12, 14, 15, 16

Alma 30: 2, 7, 8, 9, 10, 11, 20, 22, 29, 32, 33, 34, 35, 37, 39, 40, 41, 42, 44, 46, 47, 49, 50, 51, 52, 55, 56, 57, 58, 60

Alma 31: 1, 2, 5, 7, 8, 11, 24, 26, 30, 31, 32, 33, 34, 35, 37, 38

Alma 32: 1, 2, 3, 4, 5, 6, 7, 8, 9, 10, 11, 12, 14, 16, 17, 18, 19, 25, 27, 28, 30, 31, 32, 33, 34, 37, 38, 39, 40, 41

Alma 33: 1, 2, 3, 4, 5, 6, 7, 8, 9, 10, 12, 13, 14, 16, 17, 18, 19, 21

Alma 34: 3, 4, 5, 7, 8, 9, 11, 30, 31, 32, 33, 34, 35, 39, 40, 41

Alma 35: 7, 9, 14, 15, 16

Alma 36: 6, 7, 8, 9, 11, 21, 22, 23, 24, 25, 26, 29

Alma 37: 2, 3, 4, 5, 6, 7, 8, 9, 10, 11, 14, 17, 18, 19, 21, 23, 25, 26, 27, 28, 29, 30, 31, 32, 33, 34, 38, 39, 40, 41, 43, 46, 47

Alma 38: 2, 3, 4, 7, 8, 10, 11, 12

Alma 39: 1, 4, 7, 8, 9, 10, 11, 12, 13, 16, 17, 18, 19

Alma 40: 3, 4, 5, 6, 7, 8, 9, 10, 15, 17, 19, 20

Alma 41: 1, 9

Alma 42: 19, 20, 21, 29

Alma 43: 1, 9, 11, 12, 13, 23, 24, 26, 30, 45, 46, 47, 48, 49, 50, 54

Alma 44: 1, 2, 3, 4, 5, 6, 8, 11, 14, 15, 19, 20

Alma 45: 2, 3, 4, 5, 6, 7, 8, 12, 14, 15, 17, 18, 19, 20, 21, 22, 23, 24

Alma 46: 6, 7, 8, 10, 11, 12, 13, 14, 15, 16, 17, 18, 19, 20, 21, 22, 23, 24, 25, 27, 28, 30, 31, 34, 35, 36, 40

Alma 48: 7, 8, 9, 10, 11, 12, 13, 14, 17, 18, 21, 23, 24

Alma 49: 5, 9, 11, 13, 15, 20, 23, 27

Alma 50: 1, 6, 10, 11, 21, 23, 27, 36, 37, 38, 39

Alma 51: 6, 7, 14, 16, 17, 18, 20, 21, 22

Alma 52: 5, 8, 17, 19

Alma 53: 2, 5, 7, 11, 12, 13, 14, 15, 16, 17, 18, 19, 20

Alma 54: 3, 6, 7, 8, 9, 10, 11, 12, 13

Alma 55: 1, 2, 4, 8, 17, 19, 28, 31, 32

Alma 56: 8, 10, 11, 19, 45, 46, 47, 48, 56

Alma 57: 20, 21, 25, 26, 27, 35, 36

Alma 58: 8, 9, 12, 33, 37, 39

Alma 60: 3, 4, 7, 11, 13, 14, 15, 16, 20, 21, 25, 26, 28, 29, 31, 32, 33, 34, 36

Alma 61: 2, 6, 9, 10, 11, 12, 13, 14, 15, 17, 18, 19, 21

Alma 62: 1, 4, 5, 9, 10, 16, 27, 28, 29, 37, 40, 41, 42, 43, 44, 45, 46, 47, 48, 49, 50

Alma 63: 11, 12, 13

Helaman 1: 5, 6, 8, 12, 13

Helaman 2: 2, 6, 9, 10

Helaman 3: 14, 20, 21, 24, 25, 26, 31, 32, 33, 37

Helaman 4: 11, 12, 13, 14, 15, 16, 21, 22, 26

Helaman 5: 2, 5, 7, 13, 19, 24, 26, 27, 28, 29, 30, 31, 32, 33, 34, 36, 37, 38, 39, 40, 41, 42, 43, 44, 49, 50, 51, 52

Helaman 6: 1, 3, 4, 5, 6, 14, 17, 20, 34, 35, 36, 37

Helaman 7: 6, 7, 8, 9, 11, 13, 14, 15, 17, 18, 20, 22, 23, 24, 29

Helaman 8: 3, 4, 7, 8, 9, 10, 11, 12, 13, 16, 17, 19, 20, 24, 25, 27

Helaman 9: 2, 5, 10, 15, 18, 21, 22, 23, 36, 39, 40, 41

Helaman 10: 2, 8, 9, 10, 11, 12, 14, 15

Helaman 11: 4, 5, 6, 7, 8, 9, 10, 11, 12, 13, 14, 15, 16, 17, 18, 19, 20, 21, 23, 28, 34

Helaman 12: 1, 2, 3, 5, 6, 7, 8, 9, 10, 11, 12, 13, 14, 15, 16, 17, 18, 19, 20, 21, 22, 23

Helaman 13: 5, 11, 12, 13, 14, 17, 18, 19, 20, 21, 22, 23, 30, 31, 33, 34, 35, 36, 39

Helaman 14: 1, 9, 10, 11, 26, 28

Helaman 15: 1, 2, 3, 4, 5, 6, 8, 9, 10, 11, 12, 13, 15, 16, 17

Helaman 16: 1, 2, 3, 4, 5, 7, 8, 10, 14, 23

3 Nephi 1: 2, 3, 8, 10, 11, 12, 20, 22, 23, 24, 25, 26
3 Nephi 2: 8, 9, 10, 11, 12, 14, 15
3 Nephi 3: 12, 13, 14, 15, 16, 20, 21, 25, 26
3 Nephi 4: 4, 8, 10, 29, 31, 32, 33
3 Nephi 5: 1, 3, 4, 12, 14, 17, 18, 21, 22, 23
3 Nephi 6: 3, 4, 5, 6, 13, 20, 23, 25, 26
3 Nephi 7: 16, 17, 22
3 Nephi 9: 3, 4, 5, 6, 7, 8, 9, 10, 11, 12, 13, 19
3 Nephi 10: 4, 5, 6, 7, 8, 11, 12, 13, 14, 15, 17, 18, 19
3 Nephi 11: 8, 9, 13, 15, 16, 17, 18, 19, 20, 28, 29, 30, 31, 34, 41
3 Nephi 12: 2, 3, 4, 5, 6, 7, 8, 9, 10, 11, 12, 13, 14, 15, 17, 23, 24, 25, 26, 29, 30, 31, 32, 33, 34, 35, 36, 37, 38, 39, 40, 41, 42, 46, 47
3 Nephi 13: 1, 2, 3, 4, 5, 7, 16, 17, 18, 19, 20, 21, 23, 24, 25, 26, 27, 28, 29, 30, 31, 32, 34

3 Nephi 14: 3, 4, 5, 6, 9, 10, 13, 15, 16, 17, 18, 19, 20, 22, 23, 24, 25, 26, 27
3 Nephi 15: 2, 3, 4, 5, 6, 7, 8, 11, 12, 13, 14, 15, 16, 18, 19, 20, 22, 23, 24
3 Nephi 16: 1, 2, 7, 8, 9, 10, 11, 12, 13, 14, 15, 16
3 Nephi 17: 1, 2, 4, 5, 6, 7, 8, 10, 11, 12, 13, 14, 16, 17, 18, 19, 20, 21, 22, 23, 25
3 Nephi 18: 1, 2, 4, 5, 6, 7, 9, 10, 11, 12, 13, 14, 22, 25, 26, 27, 28, 29, 30, 31, 32, 33, 34, 35, 36, 38, 39
3 Nephi 19: 1, 2, 4, 19, 20, 21, 22, 24, 26, 32, 33, 34, 36
3 Nephi 20: 2, 4, 7, 11, 13, 14, 15, 18, 19, 21, 24, 28, 29, 30, 36, 40, 41, 43
3 Nephi 21: 1, 2, 4, 5, 7, 10, 22, 24, 26, 27, 28, 29
3 Nephi 22: 2, 4, 6, 7, 8, 9, 10, 11, 13, 14, 15, 16, 17
3 Nephi 23: 1, 2, 3, 4, 6, 7, 10, 11, 12, 13, 14
3 Nephi 24: 1, 9, 13, 14, 15, 16, 17
3 Nephi 25: 1, 2, 4
3 Nephi 26: 1, 6, 7, 8, 9, 10, 11, 12, 13, 16, 18, 19, 20

3 Nephi 27: 3, 4, 5, 8, 9, 10, 11, 12, 22, 23, 24, 30, 31, 32
3 Nephi 28: 2, 4, 5, 14, 16, 18, 19, 20, 21, 22, 23, 25, 26, 27, 28, 33
3 Nephi 29: 3, 4, 5, 7, 8, 9
3 Nephi 30: 2

4 Nephi 1: 2, 7, 10, 13, 14, 23, 29, 32, 33, 34, 36, 37, 44

Mormon 1: 2, 13, 16, 17, 18
Mormon 2: 13, 15, 18, 23, 24, 25, 26, 27
Mormon 3: 2, 3, 11, 14, 15, 16, 18, 19, 22
Mormon 4: 4, 5
Mormon 5: 2, 8, 10, 11, 12, 13, 15, 16, 18, 19, 20, 21, 22, 24
Mormon 6: 6, 7, 11, 16, 18, 19, 20
Mormon 7: 2, 4, 9
Mormon 8: 3, 5, 8, 11, 12, 14, 16, 18, 25, 33, 36
Mormon 9: 1, 3, 4, 8, 10, 26, 31

Ether 1: 33, 34, 35, 36, 37, 38, 39, 40, 41, 42, 43
Ether 2: 4, 5, 6, 7, 8, 9, 10, 11, 14, 18, 19, 20, 21, 22, 23, 24, 25
Ether 3: 1, 3, 5, 10, 11, 18, 21, 24
Ether 4: 1, 2, 5, 6, 8, 10, 11, 13, 14
Ether 5: 1, 6
Ether 6: 3, 4, 5, 7, 8, 9, 10, 12, 23, 25, 26, 30
Ether 7: 1, 8, 11, 23, 24, 25, 26, 27
Ether 8: 23, 24
Ether 9: 2, 3, 16, 20, 21, 22, 23, 28, 35
Ether 10: 2, 11, 13, 16, 17, 19, 28
Ether 11: 1, 6, 12, 13, 20, 21
Ether 12: 3, 4, 5, 19, 24, 25, 26, 27, 29, 35, 36
Ether 13: 2, 5, 7, 12, 13, 20, 21
Ether 14: 1, 2, 25
Ether 15: 1, 3, 11, 19, 33

Moroni 1: 4
Moroni 2: 1
Moroni 3: 1
Moroni 4: 1
Moroni 5: 1
Moroni 6: 1, 7, 8, 9
Moroni 7: 1, 3, 4, 5, 6, 7, 8, 9, 10, 11, 12, 13, 14, 15, 17, 18, 19, 20, 21, 35
Moroni 8: 2, 4, 5, 6, 10, 11, 12, 14, 19, 28, 29

Moroni 9: 4, 6, 9, 14, 15, 21, 22,
    24
Moroni 10: 22, 24, 25

Chapter Nine
The Prophecy Scriptures

The scriptures are replete with prophecies, some of which have been realized and some of which are yet to be fulfilled. Many of these prophecies aid us in preparing ourselves and our families for the forthcoming events so that we will be watchful and ready to abide the day. The following scriptures teach, or fulfil, the prophecies given by many of the prophets throughout the ages.

The Prophecy Scriptures
(Marked in Purple)

1 Nephi 1: 4, 9, 10, 11, 13, 19
1 Nephi 2: 13
1 Nephi 5: 18, 19
1 Nephi 7: 13
1 Nephi 8: 3, 4, 5, 6, 7, 8, 9, 10, 11, 12, 13, 14, 15, 16, 17, 18, 19, 20, 21, 22, 23, 24, 25, 26, 27, 28, 30, 31, 32, 33, 34, 35, 36
1 Nephi 10: 3, 4, 5, 6, 7, 8, 9, 10, 11, 12, 13, 14, 17
1 Nephi 11: 7, 8, 9, 13, 14, 15, 18, 19, 20, 21, 22, 23, 24, 25, 26, 27, 28, 29, 30, 31, 32, 33, 34, 35, 36
1 Nephi 12: 1, 2, 3, 4, 5, 6, 7, 8, 9, 10, 11, 12, 13, 14, 15, 16, 17, 18, 19, 20, 21, 22, 23

1 Nephi 13: 1, 2, 3, 4, 5, 6, 7, 8, 9, 10, 11, 12, 13, 14, 15, 16, 17, 18, 19, 20, 21, 22, 23, 24, 25, 26, 27, 28, 29, 30, 31, 32, 33, 34, 35, 36, 37, 38, 39, 40, 41, 42
1 Nephi 14: 1, 2, 3, 4, 5, 6, 7, 8, 9, 10, 11, 12, 13, 14, 15, 16, 17, 18, 19, 20, 21, 22, 23, 24, 25, 26, 27, 28
1 Nephi 15: 4, 5, 13, 14, 15, 16, 17, 18, 19, 20, 30
1 Nephi 19: 8, 9, 10, 11, 12, 13, 14, 15, 16, 17, 20, 21
1 Nephi 20: 1, 2, 3, 4, 5, 6, 7, 8, 9, 10, 11, 12, 13, 14, 15, 16, 17, 18, 19, 20, 21, 22

1 Nephi 21: 1, 2, 3, 4, 5, 6, 7, 8,
9, 10, 11, 12, 13, 14, 15, 16,
17, 18, 19, 20, 21, 22, 23, 24,
25, 26

1 Nephi 22: 3, 4, 5, 6, 7, 8, 9, 10,
11, 12, 13, 14, 15, 16, 17, 18,
19, 20, 21, 22, 23, 24, 25, 26,
27, 28

2 Nephi 1: 4, 10, 11, 12

2 Nephi 2: 3, 26

2 Nephi 3: 5, 6, 7, 8, 9, 10, 11,
12, 13, 14, 15, 16, 17, 18, 19,
20, 21, 22, 23, 24

2 Nephi 4: 1, 2, 6, 7, 9, 11

2 Nephi 6: 6, 7, 8, 9, 10, 11, 12,
13, 14, 15, 16, 17, 18

2 Nephi 7: 1, 2, 3, 4, 5, 6, 7, 8,
9, 10, 11

2 Nephi 8: 1, 2, 3, 4, 5, 6, 7, 8, 9,
10, 11, 12, 13, 14, 15, 16, 17,
18, 19, 20, 21, 22, 23, 24, 25

2 Nephi 9: 2, 5

2 Nephi 10: 2, 3, 5, 6, 7, 8, 9,
10, 11, 12, 13, 14, 15, 16, 17,
18, 19

2 Nephi 11: 7

2 Nephi 12: 1, 2, 3, 4, 5, 6, 7, 8,
9, 10, 11, 12, 13, 14, 15, 16,
17, 18, 19, 20, 21, 22

2 Nephi 13: 1, 2, 3, 4, 5, 6, 7, 8,
9, 10, 11, 12, 13, 14, 15, 16,
17, 18, 19, 20, 21, 22, 23, 24,
25, 26

2 Nephi 14: 1, 2, 3, 4, 5, 6

2 Nephi 15: 1, 2, 3, 4, 5, 6, 7, 8,
9, 10, 11, 12, 13, 14, 15, 16,
17, 18, 19, 20, 21, 22, 23, 24,
25, 26, 27, 28, 29, 30

2 Nephi 16: 1, 2, 3, 4, 5, 6, 8, 9,
10, 11, 12, 13

2 Nephi 17: 3, 4, 5, 6, 7, 8, 9, 10,
11, 12, 13, 14, 15, 16, 17, 18,
19, 20, 21, 22, 23, 24, 25

2 Nephi 18: 3, 4, 5, 6, 7, 8, 9, 10,
11, 12, 13, 14, 15, 16, 17, 18,
19, 20, 21, 22

2 Nephi 19: 1, 2, 3, 4, 5, 6, 7, 8,
9, 10, 11, 12, 13, 14, 15, 16,
17, 18, 19, 20, 21

2 Nephi 20: 1, 2, 3, 4, 5, 6, 7, 8,
9, 10, 11, 12, 13, 14, 15, 16,
17, 18, 19, 20, 21, 22, 23, 24,
25, 26, 27, 28, 29, 30, 31, 32,
33, 34

2 Nephi 21: 1, 2, 3, 4, 5, 6, 7, 8,
9, 10, 11, 12, 13, 14, 15, 16

2 Nephi 22: 1, 2, 3, 4, 5, 6

2 Nephi 23: 1, 2, 3, 4, 5, 6, 7, 8,
9, 10, 11, 12, 13, 14, 15, 16,
17, 18, 19, 20, 21, 22

2 Nephi 24: 1, 2, 3, 4, 5, 6, 7, 8,
9, 10, 11, 12, 13, 14, 15, 16,
17, 18, 19, 20, 21, 22, 23, 24,
25, 26, 27, 28, 29, 30, 31, 32

2 Nephi 25: 3, 9, 10, 11, 12, 13,
14, 15, 16, 17, 18, 19, 20, 21,
22, 26

2 Nephi 26: 1, 2, 3, 4, 5, 6, 7, 8,
9, 10, 14, 15, 16, 17, 18, 19,
20, 21, 22

2 Nephi 27: 1, 2, 3, 4, 5, 6, 7, 8,
9, 10, 11, 12, 13, 14, 15, 16,
17, 18, 19, 20, 21, 22, 23, 24,
25, 26, 27, 28, 29, 30, 31, 32,
33, 34, 35

2 Nephi 28: 1, 2, 3, 4, 5, 6, 7, 8,
9, 10, 11, 12, 13, 14, 15, 16,
17, 18, 19, 20, 21, 22, 23, 24,
25, 26, 27, 28, 29, 30, 31, 32

2 Nephi 29: 1, 2, 3, 5, 6, 13, 14

2 Nephi 30: 3, 4, 5, 6, 7, 8, 9, 10,
11, 12, 13, 14, 15, 16, 17, 18

2 Nephi 32: 6

2 Nephi 33: 11, 13, 14, 15

Jacob 1: 5, 6
Jacob 4: 4, 15, 16
Jacob 5: 29, 47, 62, 64, 69, 71,
73, 77
Jacob 6: 1, 2, 3, 4, 13

Words of Mormon 1: 4

Mosiah 3: 5, 6, 7, 8, 9, 10, 11, 15,
20, 21, 24, 25

Mosiah 4: 2, 3

Mosiah 7: 26, 27

Mosiah 13: 27, 33, 34, 35

Mosiah 14: 1, 2, 3, 4, 5, 6, 7, 8, 9,
10, 11, 12

Mosiah 15: 11, 28, 29

Mosiah 16: 1, 2

Mosiah 19: 20

Mosiah 20: 21

Mosiah 21: 4

Mosiah 26: 24, 25, 26, 27, 28

Mosiah 27: 30, 31

Alma 4: 13
Alma 5: 48, 50, 58
Alma 7: 7, 8, 9, 10, 11, 12, 13
Alma 9: 2, 3, 25, 26, 27, 28
Alma 11: 40, 41, 42, 43, 44
Alma 13: 24, 25, 26
Alma 16: 19, 20
Alma 18: 39
Alma 19: 13
Alma 21: 9
Alma 25: 9, 10, 11, 12, 15
Alma 30: 39
Alma 34: 2, 14, 37

Alma 36: 17
Alma 37: 4, 14, 18, 19
Alma 39: 15
Alma 40: 21, 22, 23, 24, 25, 26
Alma 45: 9, 10, 11, 12, 13, 14, 16

Helaman 7: 23, 24
Helaman 8: 13, 14, 15, 16, 17, 18, 19, 20, 21, 22, 27
Helaman 9: 3, 25, 26, 27, 28, 29, 30, 31, 32, 33, 34, 35, 37, 38
Helaman 12: 25, 26
Helaman 13: 5, 6, 8, 9, 10, 12, 14, 17, 18, 19, 20, 31, 32, 33, 34, 35, 36, 37
Helaman 14: 2, 3, 4, 5, 6, 7, 12, 14, 15, 20, 21, 22, 23, 24, 25, 26, 27, 28
Helaman 15: 1, 2, 11, 12, 13, 16, 17
Helaman 16: 4, 5, 13, 14

3 Nephi 1: 4, 13, 14, 15, 16, 17, 18, 19, 20, 21
3 Nephi 2: 7
3 Nephi 5: 2
3 Nephi 8: 3, 19, 20, 21, 22, 23
3 Nephi 9: 16
3 Nephi 10: 11, 14, 15, 16, 17
3 Nephi 11: 2, 10, 11, 12

3 Nephi 12: 3, 4, 5, 6, 7, 8, 9, 10, 11, 12
3 Nephi 16: 4, 5, 7, 8, 9, 10, 11, 12, 13, 14, 15, 16, 17, 18, 19, 20
3 Nephi 20: 11, 12, 13, 14, 15, 16, 17, 18, 19, 20, 21, 22, 23, 24, 25, 26, 27, 28, 29, 30, 31, 32, 33, 34, 35, 36, 37, 38, 39, 40, 41, 42, 43, 44, 45, 46
3 Nephi 21: 1, 2, 3, 4, 5, 6, 7, 8, 9, 10, 11, 12, 13, 14, 15, 16, 17, 18, 19, 20, 21, 22, 23, 24, 25, 26, 27, 28, 29
3 Nephi 22: 1, 2, 3, 4, 5, 6, 7, 8, 9, 10, 11, 12, 13, 14, 15, 16, 17
3 Nephi 23: 9, 10, 11
3 Nephi 24: 1, 2, 3, 4, 5, 6, 7, 8, 9, 10, 11, 12, 13, 14, 15, 16, 17, 18
3 Nephi 25: 1, 2, 3, 4, 5, 6
3 Nephi 26: 2, 3, 4, 5, 8, 9, 10, 11
3 Nephi 27: 11, 12, 15, 16, 17, 22, 32
3 Nephi 28: 3, 7, 8, 10, 31, 32, 33

4 Nephi 1: 49

Mormon 1: 19
Mormon 2: 10
Mormon 3: 16, 17, 18, 19, 20
Mormon 5: 8, 9, 19, 20, 23
Mormon 8: 22, 23, 25, 26, 27,
    28, 29, 30, 31, 32, 33, 34, 35,
    36, 37, 38, 39, 40, 41
Mormon 9: 2

Ether 3: 16, 24, 27, 28
Ether 4: 1, 2, 6, 7, 10, 15, 16, 17
Ether 5: 2, 3, 4, 6
Ether 7: 5
Ether 11: 6, 7
Ether 13: 3, 4, 5, 6, 7, 8, 9, 10, 11,
    12, 13, 20, 21
Ether 15: 1, 2, 3, 33

Moroni 8: 29
Moroni 10: 28, 29, 34

Chapter Ten
The Sophistries and Strategies of the Adversary Scriptures

In the *Encyclopedia of Joseph Smith's Teachings* there are 23 entries about the Savior and 25 entries about the adversary.[21] Assuredly, the Prophet Joseph Smith realized that to succeed in our mortal sojourn we not only need to take the Holy Spirit as our guide, we also need to understand how the adversary will try to deceive us with his falsehoods, half truths, and subtle ploys so we can see them coming and quickly avoid them. The following scriptures teach the sophistries and strategies of the adversary, the philosophies of men, the consequences of sin, and other negative concepts—all of which if left unchecked will lead to our demise.

The Sophistries and Strategies of the Adversary Scriptures
(Marked in Black)

1 Nephi 1: 19, 20
1 Nephi 2: 11, 12, 13, 18, 21, 23, 24
1 Nephi 3: 5, 17, 18, 25, 28, 29, 31
1 Nephi 4: 4
1 Nephi 7: 6, 7, 8, 9, 10, 11, 14, 16, 19
1 Nephi 8: 18, 20, 23, 25, 26, 27, 28, 31, 32, 33, 34, 36
1 Nephi 10: 21
1 Nephi 11: 34, 35, 36
1 Nephi 12: 16, 17, 18, 19, 21, 22, 23

1 Nephi 13: 4, 5, 6, 7, 8, 9, 26, 27, 28, 29, 32, 34
1 Nephi 14: 3, 4, 5, 6, 7, 9, 10, 11, 12, 13, 15, 16, 17
1 Nephi 15: 3, 4, 10, 24, 27, 28, 29, 33, 34, 35
1 Nephi 16: 18, 20, 22, 35, 36, 37, 38
1 Nephi 17: 17, 18, 19, 20, 21, 22, 30, 35, 41, 42, 43, 44, 45, 46, 48, 49
1 Nephi 18: 9, 10, 11, 17
1 Nephi 19: 7, 9, 13, 14
1 Nephi 20: 1, 2, 4, 5, 22
1 Nephi 21: 7

1 Nephi 22: 5, 13, 14, 15, 18, 22, 23

2 Nephi 1: 13, 17, 18, 22, 23, 24
2 Nephi 2: 1, 17, 18, 27, 29
2 Nephi 4: 13
2 Nephi 5: 1, 2, 3, 4, 14, 19, 21, 22, 23, 24
2 Nephi 6: 9, 10
2 Nephi 7: 1, 9, 10, 11
2 Nephi 8: 8
2 Nephi 9: 8, 9, 10, 16, 19, 26, 27, 28, 30, 31, 32, 33, 34, 35, 36, 37, 38, 39, 42, 45, 46, 47, 48
2 Nephi 10: 3, 5, 6
2 Nephi 12: 5, 6, 8, 9, 10, 11, 12, 17
2 Nephi 13: 11, 15, 16
2 Nephi 15: 7, 11, 12, 14, 15, 18, 19, 20, 21, 22, 23, 24
2 Nephi 17: 5, 6
2 Nephi 18: 19, 21, 22
2 Nephi 19: 9, 15, 16, 17, 18, 19, 20
2 Nephi 20: 1, 2, 12, 13, 33
2 Nephi 23: 9, 11, 15, 22
2 Nephi 24: 12, 13, 14, 15, 16, 17, 18, 19, 20, 21
2 Nephi 25: 2, 12, 13, 14, 27, 28
2 Nephi 26: 3, 4, 5, 6, 10, 20, 21, 22, 29, 32
2 Nephi 27: 1, 3, 4, 5, 14, 16, 25, 26, 27, 31, 32
2 Nephi 28: 4, 5, 6, 7, 8, 9, 10, 11, 12, 13, 14, 15, 16, 17, 18, 19, 20, 21, 22, 23, 24, 25, 26, 27, 28, 29, 31
2 Nephi 30: 9, 10
2 Nephi 32: 7, 8
2 Nephi 33: 2, 5

Jacob 1: 15, 16
Jacob 2: 5, 10, 13, 14, 16, 20, 22, 23, 24, 31, 32, 33, 34, 35
Jacob 3: 3, 4, 5, 9, 10, 11, 12
Jacob 4: 14
Jacob 5: 7, 9, 40, 42, 44, 45, 47, 48, 49, 58, 66, 69, 73, 74, 75, 77
Jacob 6: 3, 4, 8, 9, 10, 13
Jacob 7: 2, 3, 4, 6, 7, 9, 13, 18, 19, 20, 24

Enos 1: 10, 14, 20

Jarom 1: 3, 6

Omni 1: 2, 5, 6, 7, 10, 17, 25, 28

Words of Mormon 1: 12, 15, 16, 17

Mosiah 1: 17
Mosiah 2: 32, 33, 36, 37, 38, 39, 40
Mosiah 3: 6, 9, 12, 14, 15, 25, 26, 27
Mosiah 4: 14, 29
Mosiah 7: 21, 22, 24, 25, 26, 28, 29, 30, 31, 32
Mosiah 8: 20, 21
Mosiah 9: 10, 12, 13, 14
Mosiah 10: 6, 14, 15, 16, 17, 18
Mosiah 11: 2, 4, 5, 6, 7, 11, 14, 15, 16, 17, 19, 20, 21, 22, 23, 24, 25, 26, 27, 28, 29
Mosiah 12: 1, 2, 3, 4, 5, 6, 7, 8, 9, 10, 11, 12, 13, 14, 15, 16, 17, 18, 19, 26, 29, 32
Mosiah 13: 1, 11, 29
Mosiah 15: 26
Mosiah 16: 2, 3, 5, 11, 12
Mosiah 17: 1, 3, 7, 8, 12, 13, 14, 16, 17, 18
Mosiah 19: 11
Mosiah 20: 5
Mosiah 21: 30
Mosiah 23: 12, 37
Mosiah 24: 5, 7, 8, 9, 11
Mosiah 26: 2, 3, 4, 6, 27
Mosiah 27: 1, 8, 9, 10, 11
Mosiah 29: 7, 9, 17, 18, 21, 22, 23, 27, 30, 31, 35, 36, 40

Alma 1: 3, 4, 5, 6, 7, 9, 12, 15, 16, 17, 19, 20, 22, 24, 32
Alma 2: 1, 2, 4, 8, 9, 10, 14, 27
Alma 3: 2, 6, 10, 13, 18, 26
Alma 4: 6, 7, 8, 9, 10, 11, 12, 15, 19
Alma 5: 7, 9, 17, 18, 20, 22, 23, 25, 30, 32, 36, 37, 38, 39, 40, 41, 42, 53, 54, 55, 56
Alma 6: 3
Alma 7: 6, 15, 21
Alma 8: 9, 11, 12, 13, 17, 28
Alma 9: 4, 5, 6, 8, 11, 18, 19, 28, 30, 31, 32
Alma 10: 6, 13, 14, 16, 17, 18, 19, 24, 25, 27, 28, 29, 30, 31, 32
Alma 11: 20, 21, 22, 23, 24, 25, 26, 28, 30, 32, 34, 35, 38
Alma 12: 3, 4, 5, 6, 10, 11, 13, 14, 17, 18, 35, 36
Alma 13: 4, 17, 20, 30
Alma 14: 2, 3, 5, 6, 7, 8, 9, 11, 14, 15, 16, 19, 20, 21, 22, 24, 25, 27, 28
Alma 15: 3, 15, 17
Alma 16: 17, 18
Alma 17: 14, 15
Alma 18: 5, 6, 7
Alma 19: 19, 20, 21, 22, 26
Alma 20: 10, 13, 14, 16, 18, 19, 20, 30

Alma 21: 3, 5, 6, 8, 10, 12
Alma 22: 19, 21, 22, 24
Alma 23: 14
Alma 24: 1, 2, 4, 7, 20, 25, 28, 30
Alma 25: 4, 7, 8
Alma 26: 13, 14, 15, 17, 18, 19, 20, 23, 24, 25, 29
Alma 27: 2, 12, 23
Alma 28: 13
Alma 30: 6, 10, 12, 13, 14, 15, 16, 17, 18, 23, 24, 25, 26, 27, 28, 29, 30, 31, 36, 38, 42, 43, 44, 45, 46, 47, 48, 52, 53, 54, 56, 59, 60
Alma 31: 1, 9, 11, 12, 13, 14, 15, 16, 17, 18, 20, 21, 22, 23, 24, 25, 27, 28, 29
Alma 32: 3, 5
Alma 33: 17, 20, 21
Alma 34: 23, 31, 35, 39
Alma 35: 3, 5, 6, 8, 10, 11, 15
Alma 36: 6, 11, 12, 13, 14, 15, 16, 17, 18
Alma 37: 10, 15, 21, 22, 23, 25, 26, 27, 28, 29, 30, 31, 33, 42
Alma 38: 11, 13
Alma 39: 1, 2, 3, 4, 5, 6, 7, 11
Alma 40: 13, 14, 15, 26
Alma 41: 4, 5, 11
Alma 42: 1, 28

Alma 43: 6, 7, 8, 10, 11, 29
Alma 44: 2, 9, 16
Alma 45: 12, 23, 24
Alma 46: 1, 2, 3, 4, 5, 6, 7, 8, 9, 10
Alma 47: 1, 4, 8, 13, 14, 15, 16, 17, 18, 19, 22, 23, 24, 25, 26, 27, 28, 30, 31, 32, 34, 35, 36
Alma 48: 1, 2, 3, 4, 5, 7, 24
Alma 49: 7, 10, 13, 26, 27
Alma 50: 21, 22, 26, 30, 35
Alma 51: 4, 5, 8, 9, 13, 17, 18, 21
Alma 53: 9
Alma 54: 7, 8, 9, 10, 11, 13, 16, 17, 18, 21, 22, 24
Alma 59: 11, 12
Alma 60: 15, 16, 17, 32
Alma 61: 4
Alma 62: 2, 9, 10, 40
Alma 63: 14

Helaman 1: 7, 8, 9, 11, 12, 15, 16, 17, 18, 20, 21, 27
Helaman 2: 3, 4, 5, 7, 8, 9, 11, 13
Helaman 3: 1, 3, 14, 16, 17, 19, 23, 29, 33, 34, 36
Helaman 4: 1, 2, 3, 4, 5, 11, 12, 13, 21, 22, 23, 25, 26
Helaman 5: 2, 3, 12, 35

Helaman 6: 2, 15, 16, 17, 18, 19, 20, 21, 22, 23, 24, 25, 26, 27, 28, 29, 30, 31, 32, 33, 34, 35, 38, 39, 40

Helaman 7: 3, 4, 5, 6, 9, 11, 14, 15, 16, 18, 19, 21, 22, 24, 25, 26, 27, 28

Helaman 8: 1, 2, 4, 5, 6, 7, 24, 25, 26, 27, 28

Helaman 9: 2, 6, 16, 17, 19, 20, 21, 22, 23, 24, 27, 28, 29, 30

Helaman 10: 3, 13, 15, 18

Helaman 11: 1, 2, 23, 24, 25, 26, 27, 31, 32, 33, 34, 36, 37

Helaman 12: 1, 2, 4, 5, 6, 18, 20, 21, 22, 26

Helaman 13: 1, 2, 8, 12, 14, 15, 16, 17, 20, 21, 22, 23, 24, 25, 26, 27, 28, 29, 30, 31, 32, 33, 37, 38

Helaman 14: 10, 11

Helaman 15: 4

Helaman 16: 2, 6, 10, 12, 15, 16, 17, 18, 19, 20, 21, 22, 23

3 Nephi 1: 6, 7, 9, 16, 22, 27, 28, 29, 30

3 Nephi 2: 1, 2, 3, 10, 11, 13, 17, 18, 19

3 Nephi 3: 7, 8, 9, 10

3 Nephi 4: 5

3 Nephi 5: 5, 6

3 Nephi 6: 10, 12, 13, 14, 15, 16, 17, 18, 20, 21, 23, 25, 27, 28, 29, 30

3 Nephi 7: 1, 2, 5, 6, 7, 8, 9, 10, 11, 12, 14, 15, 16, 18, 19, 20

3 Nephi 8: 8, 9, 10, 14, 15, 16, 24, 25

3 Nephi 9: 2, 3, 4, 5, 6, 7, 8, 9, 10, 11, 12

3 Nephi 11: 29, 30, 40

3 Nephi 13: 2, 5, 7, 16, 23

3 Nephi 14: 13, 15, 17, 18, 19, 23

3 Nephi 16: 10

3 Nephi 18: 13, 15, 18

3 Nephi 20: 28

3 Nephi 21: 10

3 Nephi 24: 5, 14, 15

3 Nephi 27: 11, 32, 33

3 Nephi 29: 5, 6, 7

3 Nephi 30: 2

4 Nephi 1: 24, 26, 27, 28, 29, 30, 31, 32, 33, 34, 35, 38, 39, 40, 41, 42, 43, 45, 46, 47

Mormon 1: 13, 14, 16, 17, 18, 19

Mormon 2: 8, 10, 13, 14, 15, 18, 19, 27

Mormon 3: 3, 9, 10, 11, 12, 13, 14, 15
Mormon 4: 5, 8, 10, 11, 12, 14, 15, 21
Mormon 5: 2, 15, 18
Mormon 6: 7, 8
Mormon 8: 8, 9, 21, 27, 28, 31, 32, 33, 36, 37, 38, 39, 40, 41
Mormon 9: 3, 4, 7, 8, 14, 26

Ether 4: 15
Ether 7: 4, 15, 23, 24
Ether 8: 2, 3, 7, 8, 9, 10, 11, 12, 13, 14, 15, 16, 17, 18, 19, 20, 21, 22, 23, 24, 25
Ether 9: 1, 4, 5, 6, 7, 10, 11, 12, 26, 27, 29, 30
Ether 10: 3, 5, 6, 7, 8, 9, 11, 13, 33
Ether 11: 2, 5, 6, 7, 10, 11, 13, 14, 15, 22
Ether 13: 15, 16, 17, 18, 22, 25, 26, 31
Ether 14: 1, 8, 9, 10, 17, 18, 21, 22, 23, 24, 25, 27
Ether 15: 2, 6, 16, 17, 19, 22

Moroni 1: 2
Moroni 7: 12, 17
Moroni 8: 9, 13, 14, 15, 20, 21, 23, 27, 28

Moroni 9: 3, 4, 5, 6, 8, 9, 10, 13, 15, 17, 18, 19, 20, 22, 23
Moroni 10: 22

Chapter Eleven
The Informational Scriptures

All of the previous chapters have detailed some doctrine or principle, positive or negative, to aid us in understanding the teachings of the kingdom or the dangers of the devil. This chapter lists all of the remaining verses, which tend to be informational rather than doctrinal. The following scriptures are informational scriptures.

The Informational Scriptures
(Marked in Brown)

1 Nephi 1: 2, 3, 17
1 Nephi 2: 4, 5, 6, 8
1 Nephi 3: 1, 3, 4, 9, 10, 11, 12, 13, 14, 22, 23, 24, 26, 27, 30
1 Nephi 4: 5, 7, 8, 9, 16, 17, 19, 20, 21, 22, 23, 24, 25, 26, 27, 28, 29, 30, 35, 36, 38
1 Nephi 5: 1, 2, 3, 11, 12, 13, 15, 16
1 Nephi 6: 1, 2, 3
1 Nephi 7: 2, 3
1 Nephi 8: 1, 29
1 Nephi 9: 1, 2, 4
1 Nephi 10: 1, 15, 16
1 Nephi 11: 12
1 Nephi 15: 1, 2, 7
1 Nephi 16: 6, 11, 12, 13, 14, 15, 16, 17, 19, 21, 30, 31, 33, 34
1 Nephi 17: 1, 4, 6, 24, 25, 26, 27, 28

1 Nephi 18: 7, 8, 13, 14, 22, 23, 25
1 Nephi 22: 29

2 Nephi 4: 8, 10, 14
2 Nephi 5: 7, 8, 9, 12, 13, 28, 29, 33, 34
2 Nephi 6: 1
2 Nephi 9: 54
2 Nephi 11: 1, 8
2 Nephi 17: 1, 2
2 Nephi 18: 1, 2
2 Nephi 25: 1
2 Nephi 31: 1

Jacob 1: 1, 3, 9, 11, 12, 13, 14
Jacob 2: 1, 12
Jacob 3: 13, 14
Jacob 4: 1, 2
Jacob 5: 1, 6, 21, 55, 56, 67

Jacob 7: 1, 16

Enos 1: 21, 24, 25

Jarom 1: 1, 2, 8, 13, 14, 15

Omni 1: 1, 3, 4, 8, 9, 11, 14, 15, 16, 18, 19, 21, 23, 24, 27, 29, 30

Words of Mormon 1: 1, 2, 3, 5, 6, 10, 13

Mosiah 1: 1, 8, 9, 10, 14, 15
Mosiah 2: 2, 5, 6, 7, 29
Mosiah 3: 1
Mosiah 6: 4, 5
Mosiah 7: 1, 2, 3, 4, 5, 6, 7, 8, 9, 10, 11, 14, 15, 17, 23
Mosiah 8: 1, 2, 3, 4, 5, 6, 7, 8, 9, 10, 11, 12
Mosiah 9: 1, 2, 4, 5, 6, 7, 8, 9, 11, 16, 19
Mosiah 10: 1, 3, 4, 5, 8, 9, 12, 20, 21
Mosiah 11: 1, 3, 8, 9, 10, 12, 13, 18
Mosiah 12: 20, 28
Mosiah 17: 5, 6
Mosiah 18: 4, 5, 6, 31, 32, 33, 34, 35

Mosiah 19: 1, 2, 3, 4, 5, 6, 7, 8, 9, 10, 12, 13, 14, 15, 16, 17, 18, 19, 21, 22, 23, 24, 25, 26, 27, 28, 29
Mosiah 20: 1, 2, 3, 4, 6, 7, 8, 9, 10, 12, 13, 15, 16, 18, 19, 20, 23, 25
Mosiah 21: 1, 2, 3, 5, 7, 8, 9, 10, 11, 12, 16, 18, 19, 20, 21, 22, 23, 24, 25, 26, 27, 28, 29, 36
Mosiah 22: 2, 5, 6, 7, 8, 9, 10, 11, 12, 13, 15, 16
Mosiah 23: 3, 4, 20, 25, 26, 30, 31, 32, 33, 35, 36, 38, 39
Mosiah 24: 1, 2, 3, 4, 18, 20, 24, 25
Mosiah 25: 1, 2, 3, 4, 5, 6, 7, 13, 14
Mosiah 26: 1, 5, 7, 9
Mosiah 27: 2, 6, 12, 19, 34
Mosiah 28: 8, 9, 10, 11, 12, 17, 18, 19
Mosiah 29: 1, 2, 3, 4, 6, 44, 46, 47

Alma 1: 2, 11, 18, 23, 28
Alma 2: 11, 13, 15, 17, 19, 20, 22, 23, 24, 25, 26, 29, 32, 33, 34, 35, 36, 37, 38
Alma 3: 1, 3, 4, 5, 20, 21, 22, 23, 25

Alma 4: 1, 2, 17
Alma 5: 2, 8
Alma 6: 4, 7
Alma 7: 1, 18
Alma 8: 1, 2, 3, 5, 6, 7, 27
Alma 9: 34
Alma 10: 1, 2, 3, 4, 15
Alma 11: 1, 2, 3, 4, 5, 6, 7, 8, 9,
    10, 11, 12, 13, 14, 15, 16, 17,
    18, 19
Alma 12: 2, 19
Alma 13: 31
Alma 14: 4, 12
Alma 15: 1, 4, 19
Alma 16: 1, 2, 3, 4, 7, 8, 11, 12
Alma 17: 1, 7, 19, 20, 21, 22, 24,
    26, 27, 28, 32, 33, 34, 37, 38,
    39
Alma 18: 1, 2, 4, 8, 11, 13, 21,
    37, 42, 43
Alma 19: 1, 2, 3, 5, 7, 8, 11, 18,
    28
Alma 20: 6, 8, 9, 11, 12, 23
Alma 21: 1, 2, 4, 13, 18
Alma 22: 2, 27, 28, 29, 30, 31,
    32, 33, 34, 35
Alma 23: 2, 9, 10, 11, 12, 13, 16,
    17
Alma 24: 3
Alma 25: 1, 2, 3, 5, 13
Alma 27: 1, 3, 5, 6, 14, 20, 25,
    26, 29
Alma 28: 1, 2, 3, 4, 5, 7, 9, 10
Alma 30: 1, 4, 5, 19, 21
Alma 31: 3, 4, 6, 19
Alma 32: 24
Alma 33: 15
Alma 34: 1
Alma 35: 1, 2, 4, 12, 13
Alma 36: 10
Alma 37: 1, 24
Alma 40: 1
Alma 43: 3, 4, 5, 14, 15, 16, 17,
    18, 19, 20, 21, 22, 25, 27, 28,
    31, 32, 33, 34, 35, 36, 37, 38,
    39, 40, 41, 42, 43, 44, 51, 52,
    53
Alma 44: 7, 10, 12, 13, 17, 18,
    21, 22, 23, 24
Alma 46: 26, 29, 32, 33, 37, 38
Alma 47: 2, 3, 5, 6, 7, 9, 10, 11,
    12, 20, 21, 29, 33
Alma 48: 6, 22
Alma 49: 1, 2, 3, 4, 6, 8, 12, 14,
    16, 17, 18, 19, 21, 22, 24, 25,
    29
Alma 50: 2, 3, 4, 5, 7, 8, 9, 12,
    13, 14, 15, 16, 17, 18, 24, 25,
    28, 29, 31, 32, 33, 34, 40
Alma 51: 1, 2, 3, 10, 11, 12, 15,
    19, 23, 24, 25, 26, 27, 28, 29,
    30, 31, 32, 33, 34, 35, 36, 37

Alma 52: 1, 2, 3, 4, 6, 7, 9, 10, 11, 12, 13, 14, 15, 16, 18, 20, 21, 22, 23, 24, 25, 26, 27, 28, 29, 30, 31, 32, 33, 34, 35, 36, 37, 38, 39, 40

Alma 53: 1, 3, 4, 6, 8, 22, 23

Alma 54: 1, 2, 4, 5, 14, 15, 19, 20, 23

Alma 55: 3, 5, 6, 7, 9, 10, 11, 12, 13, 14, 15, 16, 18, 20, 21, 22, 23, 24, 25, 26, 27, 29, 30, 33, 34, 35

Alma 56: 1, 2, 3, 4, 5, 6, 7, 9, 12, 13, 14, 15, 16, 17, 18, 20, 21, 22, 23, 24, 25, 26, 27, 28, 29, 30, 31, 32, 33, 34, 35, 36, 37, 38, 39, 40, 41, 42, 43, 44, 49, 50, 51, 52, 53, 54, 55, 57

Alma 57: 1, 2, 3, 4, 5, 6, 7, 8, 9, 10, 11, 12, 13, 14, 15, 16, 17, 18, 19, 22, 23, 24, 28, 29, 30, 31, 32, 33, 34

Alma 58: 1, 2, 3, 4, 5, 6, 7, 13, 14, 15, 16, 17, 18, 19, 20, 21, 22, 23, 24, 25, 26, 27, 28, 29, 30, 31, 32, 34, 35, 36, 38

Alma 59: 1, 2, 3, 4, 5, 6, 7, 8, 9, 10, 13

Alma 60: 1, 2, 5, 6, 8, 9, 10, 12, 18, 19, 22, 24, 27, 30, 35

Alma 61: 1, 3, 5, 7, 8, 16

Alma 62: 3, 6, 7, 8, 11, 12, 13, 14, 15, 17, 18, 19, 20, 21, 22, 23, 24, 25, 26, 30, 31, 32, 33, 34, 35, 36, 38, 39, 52

Alma 63: 1, 3, 4, 5, 6, 7, 8, 9, 10, 15, 16, 17

Helaman 1: 1, 2, 3, 4, 10, 14, 19, 22, 23, 24, 25, 26, 28, 29, 30, 31, 32, 33, 34

Helaman 2: 1, 12, 14

Helaman 3: 2, 4, 5, 6, 7, 8, 9, 10, 11, 12, 13, 15, 18, 22

Helaman 4: 6, 7, 8, 9, 10, 17, 18, 19, 20

Helaman 5: 1, 15, 16, 20, 21, 22, 25

Helaman 6: 7, 8, 9, 10, 11, 12, 13, 41

Helaman 7: 1, 10, 12

Helaman 9: 1, 4, 7, 8, 9, 11, 12, 13, 14

Helaman 10: 1, 19

Helaman 11: 22, 29, 30, 35, 38

Helaman 16: 9, 11, 24, 25

3 Nephi 1: 1, 5

3 Nephi 2: 4, 5, 6, 16

3 Nephi 3: 1, 2, 3, 4, 5, 6, 11, 17, 18, 22, 23, 24

3 Nephi 4: 1, 2, 3, 6, 7, 9, 11, 12, 13, 14, 15, 16, 17, 18, 19, 20, 21, 22, 23, 24, 25, 26, 27, 28

3 Nephi 5: 7, 8, 9, 10, 11, 15, 16, 19

3 Nephi 6: 1, 2, 7, 8, 9, 11, 19, 22, 24

3 Nephi 7: 3, 4, 13

3 Nephi 8: 2, 4, 5, 6, 7, 11, 12, 13, 17, 18

3 Nephi 10: 1, 2, 9

3 Nephi 11: 1

3 Nephi 18: 17

3 Nephi 19: 3, 5

3 Nephi 20: 6

3 Nephi 23: 8

3 Nephi 28: 24

4 Nephi 1: 4, 6, 8, 9, 19, 20, 21, 22, 25

Mormon 1: 1, 3, 4, 5, 6, 7, 8, 9, 10, 11, 12

Mormon 2: 1, 2, 3, 4, 5, 6, 7, 9, 11, 16, 17, 20, 21, 22, 28, 29

Mormon 3: 1, 4, 5, 6, 7, 8

Mormon 4: 1, 2, 3, 6, 7, 9, 13, 16, 17, 18, 19, 20, 22, 23

Mormon 5: 1, 3, 4, 5, 6, 7

Mormon 6: 1, 2, 3, 4, 5, 9, 10, 12, 13, 14, 15

Mormon 7: 1

Mormon 8: 1, 2, 4, 6, 7, 13

Mormon 9: 30, 32, 33, 34

Ether 1: 1, 2, 3, 4, 5, 6, 7, 8, 9, 10, 11, 12, 13, 14, 15, 16, 17, 18, 19, 20, 21, 22, 23, 24, 25, 26, 27, 28, 29, 30, 31, 32

Ether 2: 1, 2, 3, 13, 16, 17

Ether 3: 22, 23

Ether 4: 3, 4

Ether 6: 1, 2, 6, 11, 13, 14, 15, 16, 18, 19, 20, 21, 22, 24, 27, 28, 29

Ether 7: 2, 3, 6, 7, 9, 10, 12, 14, 16, 17, 18, 19, 20, 21, 22

Ether 8: 1, 4, 5, 6

Ether 9: 8, 9, 13, 14, 15, 17, 18, 19, 24, 25, 31, 32, 33

Ether 10: 1, 4, 10, 12, 14, 15, 18, 20, 21, 22, 23, 24, 25, 26, 27, 29, 30, 31, 32, 34

Ether 11: 3, 4, 9, 16, 17, 18, 19, 23

Ether 12: 1, 40

Ether 13: 1, 14, 19, 23, 24, 27, 28, 29, 30

Ether 14: 3, 4, 5, 6, 7, 11, 12, 13, 14, 15, 16, 19, 20, 26, 28, 29, 30, 31

Ether 15: 4, 5, 7, 8, 9, 10, 12, 13,
    14, 15, 18, 20, 21, 23, 24, 25,
    26, 27, 28, 29, 30, 31, 32

Moroni 1: 1
Moroni 8: 1, 30
Moroni 9: 1, 2, 7, 11, 12, 16
Moroni 10: 1, 2

Chapter Twelve
Gospel Scholarship

Perhaps the primary benefit of gospel scholarship is revelation from God through the Holy Ghost. Elder Dallin H. Oaks teaches that "in the acquisition of sacred knowledge, scholarship and reason are not alternatives to revelation. They are a means to an end, and the end is revelation from God."[22] Joseph Smith taught that "no man can receive the Holy Ghost without receiving revelations. The Holy Ghost is a revelator."[23] The Holy Ghost's commission is to act as our constant companion, our scepter–a royal authority–of righteousness and truth.[24] Hence, the Holy Ghost knows all things,[25] can show us all things,[26] can teach us all things,[27] and can manifest to us the truth of all things.[28] Moreover, he will bring all things to our remembrance[29] and will show us all things that we should do.[30]

As a member of the Godhead, part of the Holy Ghost's duty to those of us who have received the gift of the Holy Ghost is to train and tutor us, precept by precept,[31] day by day, how to become like God. He will teach us how to go from who we are and where we are, to who we need to become and where we need to go—so that as "true followers" of Jesus Christ, we "may become the sons [and daughters] of God; that when he shall appear we shall be like him."[32] I believe the Lord intends us to have the Holy Ghost as our constant companion for this very purpose: to become God-like.

The Holy Ghost's influence is remarkable. Sheri L. Dew teaches that "the Holy Ghost enlarges our minds, our hearts, and our understanding; helps us subdue weaknesses and resist temptation; inspires humility and repentance; guides and protects us in miraculous ways; and gifts us with wisdom, divine encouragement, peace of mind, a desire to change, and the ability to differentiate between the philosophies of men and revealed truth. . . . Without the presence of the Spirit, it is impossible to comprehend our personal mission or to have the reassurance that our course is right."[33]

Parley P. Pratt taught that "an intelligent being, in the image of God, possesses every organ, attribute, sense, sympathy, affection, that is possessed by God himself. . . . The gift of the Holy Ghost adapts itself to all these organs or attributes. It quickens all the intellectual faculties, increases, enlarges, expands and purifies all the natural passions and affections, and adapts them, by the gift of wisdom, to their lawful use. It inspires, develops, cultivates and matures all the fine-toned sympathies, joys, tastes, kindred feelings and affections of our nature. It inspires virtue, kindness, goodness, tenderness, gentleness and charity. It develops beauty of person, form and features. It tends to health, vigor, animation and social feeling. It invigorates all the faculties of the physical and intellectual man. It strengthens and gives tone to the nerves. In short, it is, as it were, marrow to the bone, joy to the heart, light to the eyes, music to the ears, and life to the whole being."[34]

The Holy Ghost can speak to each of us in many different ways. Although he has spoken to me in a variety of ways, the manner in which he speaks to me most often is by softly placing a thought in the back of my mind, gently prompting me to act upon that thought and do the expedient thing of the moment or the day.[35] And his Spirit just stays there nudging me along until I do it. He is so constant, so subtle, so quiet.

A secondary benefit of gospel scholarship is the acquisition of a knowledge of the doctrines and principles of the kingdom. We can apply this knowledge in the practicum of our lives as we journey toward heaven. Such knowledge is applicable in all aspects of life and most applicable in family life, for that is where we practice for eternal life—eternal family life. For such reasons the prophets have said: "We must work at our responsibility as parents as if everything in life counted on it, because in fact everything in life does count on it. If we fail in our homes, we fail in our lives;"[36] The greatest work you will ever do will be within the walls of your own home;[37] and "No other success can compensate for failure in the home."[38]

Additional benefits flow from gospel scholarship. Spiritual protection seems to rest upon us as we read and study the scriptures. Perhaps we do not fully understand how spiritually protective scripture study can be in our lives. Also, both discernment and judgement–two remarkable and almost indispensable qualities needed in our day–seem to progressively increase in our lives as we diligently study the scriptures. Moreover, Christ's pure love, and our pure love of Christ, deepens in our souls as we read and ponder the scriptures. When the love of the Savior burns in our hearts, the desire to do every good thing permeates our beings.

Furthermore, gospel scholarship specifically in the Book of Mormon has its unique rewards and contributions to our lives. Consider these thoughts and promises from latter day prophets, seers, and revelators:

Gordon B. Hinckley – "Without reservation I promise you that if you will prayerfully read the Book of Mormon...there will come into your hearts an added measure of the Spirit of the Lord. There will come a strengthened resolution to walk in obedience to his commandments, and there will come a stronger testimony of the living reality of the Son of God."[39]

Russell M. Nelson – "Each individual who prayerfully studies the Book of Mormon can also receive a testimony of its divinity. In addition, this book can help with personal problems in a very real way. Do you want to get rid of a bad habit? Do you want to improve relationships in your family? Do you want to increase your spiritual capacity? Read the Book of Mormon! It will bring you closer to the Lord and his loving power. He who fed a multitude with five loaves and two fishes—He who helped the blind to see and the lame to walk—can also bless you! He has promised that those who live by the precepts of this book 'shall receive a crown of eternal life.'"[40]

Richard G. Scott – "It is not sufficient that we should treasure the Book of Mormon, nor that we testify that it is of God. We must know its truths, incorporate them into our lives, and share them with others."[41]

Ezra Taft Benson – "Every Latter-day Saint should make the study of [the Book of Mormon] a lifetime pursuit. Otherwise he is placing his soul in jeopardy and neglecting that which could give spiritual and intellectual unity to his whole life. . . . It will hold us as close to the Spirit of the Lord as anything I know."[42]

Ezra Taft Benson – "Members of the Church everywhere should know the Book of Mormon better than any other book. . . . I have noted within the Church the difference in discernment, in insight, conviction, and spirit between those who know and love the Book of Mormon and those who do not. That book is a great sifter."[43]

Ezra Taft Benson – "I bless you with increased *understanding* of the Book of Mormon. I promise you that from this moment forward, if we will daily sup from its pages and abide by its precepts, God will pour out upon each child of Zion and the Church a blessing hitherto unknown."[44]

Ezra Taft Benson – "Young men, the Book of Mormon will change your life. It will fortify you against the evils of our day. It will bring a spirituality into your life that no other book will. . . . A young man who knows and loves the Book of Mormon . . . and who applies its teachings will be able to stand against the wiles of the devil and will be a mighty tool in the hands of the Lord."[45]

Ezra Taft Benson – "There is a power in the [Book of Mormon] which will begin to flow into your lives the moment you begin a serious study of the book. You will find greater power to resist temptation. You will find the power to avoid deception. You will find the power to stay on the strait and narrow path."[46]

Marion G. Romney – "I feel certain that if, in our homes, parents will read from the Book of Mormon prayerfully and regularly, both by themselves and with their children, the spirit of that great book will come to permeate our homes and all who dwell therein. The spirit of reverence will increase; mutual respect and consideration for each other will grow. The spirit of contention will depart. Parents will counsel their children in greater love and wisdom. Children will be more responsive and submissive to the counsel of their parents. Righteousness will increase. Faith, hope, and charity–the pure love of Christ–will abound in our homes and lives, bringing in their wake peace, joy, and happiness."[47]

Joseph Smith Jr. – "I told the brethren that the Book of Mormon was the most correct of any book on earth, and the keystone of our religion, and a man would get nearer to God by abiding by its precepts, than by any other book."[48]

Finally, consider the words of Daniel H. Ludlow, former dean of religious education at Brigham Young University and editor-in-chief of the *Encyclopedia of Mormonism*:

> I honestly believe, my dear brothers and sisters, that at
> the final judgment we will give our accountability as to
> what we have done with the Book of Mormon and its
> teachings. I believe the questions will be asked of us in
> about the following order, and the first time we have to
> answer "no" will be the point of our judgment.
>
> 1. Did you have opportunity to read the Book of
> Mormon while you lived on the earth? (All of us reading
> this would have to answer this question "Yes.")
>
> 2. Did you read the Book of Mormon?
>
> 3. Did you learn the great principles of righteousness
> contained in the Book of Mormon?
>
> 4. Did you apply these principles in you life?
>
> 5. Did you teach these principles to your children and to
> others?
>
> It may be that if we can honestly answer "yes" to all
> of these questions, we might then hear those gladsome
> words, "Well done, thou good and faithful servant: . . .
> enter thou into the joy of thy Lord" (Matthew 25:21). . . .
> May we learn it, and love it—and live it.[49]

Thank you for being such a willing student of the Book of
Mormon. You will have the most extraordinary constant companion in

the Holy Ghost. You will become a truly fine gospel scholar. You will have an increase in spiritual protection, discernment, and judgement in your life. You will be filled more abundantly with Christ's pure love and have a greater love for him. You will receive the blessings promised by the prophets, seers, and revelators. And lastly, you will be able to make the great principles taught within the Book of Mormon more fully a part of your life. All of these opportunities will be yours as you read and study the Book of Mormon. *Make Your Mark in the Scriptures -In- the Book of Mormon* will help you in this reading and studying to realize all these benefits and blessings. Good luck to you. May the heavens bless you.

Mark Hale

Notes

1. *The Book of Mormon*, Introduction, Salt Lake City: The Church of Jesus Christ of Latter-day Saints, 1981.

2. See 3 Nephi 27: 25-26.

3. Boyd K. Packer, "'Learn of me,' Savior said," *LDS Church News*, January 4, 2003, p. 16.

4. See 1 Nephi 1: 11-12.

5. See 1 Nephi 2: 19; 1 Nephi 10: 17; 1 Nephi 5: 21.

6. Mosiah 4: 3, see also 2 Nephi 9: 23.

7. Moroni 7: 25.

8. Moroni 7: 40.

9. Alma 32: 21, see also Ether 12: 6.

10. Ether 12: 6.

11. Moroni 7: 43, see also Moroni 7: 39.

12. Moroni 7: 44.

13. Moroni 7: 28, see also Moroni 7: 25.

14. Moroni 7: 24.

15. *Lectures on Faith* (7:3), comp. N. B. Lundwall, Salt Lake City: Bookcraft, p. 61.

16. 2 Nephi 24: 24.

17. Hebrews 11: 3.

18. Mormon 9: 21, see also Mormon 9: 25.

19. James 1: 6-7.

20. 3 Nephi 12: 48.

21. *Encyclopedia of Joseph Smith's Teachings*, Larry E. Dahl and Donald Q. Cannon, eds., Salt Lake City: Deseret Book Co., 2000, p. ix. (Formerly titled *The Teachings of Joseph Smith*, Salt Lake City: Bookcraft, 1997.)

22. Dallin H. Oaks, "Alternate Voices," *Ensign*, May 1989, p 30.

23. *Teachings of the Prophet Joseph Smith*, comp. Joseph Fielding Smith, Salt Lake City: Deseret Book Co., 1976, p. 328.

24. See D&C 121: 46.

25. See D&C 35: 19.

26. See D&C 39: 6.

27. See John 14: 26.

28. See Moroni 10: 4-5.

29. See John 14: 26.

30. See 2 Nephi 32: 5.

31. See D&C 98: 12.

32. Moroni 7: 48, see also 1 John 3: 2.

33. Sheri L. Dew, "We Are Not Alone," *Ensign*, November 1998, p. 95.

34. Parley P. Pratt, *Key to the Science of Theology*, Salt Lake City: Deseret Book Co., 1948, pp. 99-100.

35. See D&C 18: 18.

36. Gordon B. Hinckley, "Each a Better Person," *Ensign*, November 2002, p. 100.

37. Harold B. Lee, "Follow the Leadership of the Church," *Ensign*, July 1973, p. 98.

38. *The Teachings of David O. McKay*, comp. Mary Jane Woodger, Salt Lake City: Deseret Book Co., 2004, p. 404.

39. Gordon B. Hinckley, "The Power of the Book of Mormon," *Ensign*, June 1988, p. 6.

40. Russell M. Nelson, "A Testimony of the Book of Mormon," *Ensign*, November 1999, p. 71.

41. Richard G. Scott, "True Friends That Lift," *Ensign*, November 1988, p. 76.

42. Ezra Taft Benson, "The Book of Mormon Is the Word of God," *Ensign*, May 1975, p. 65.

43. Ezra Taft Benson, "Jesus Christ – Gifts and Expectations," *New Era*, May 1975, p. 19.

44. Ezra Taft Benson, "A Sacred Responsibility," *Ensign,* May 1986, p. 78.

45. Ezra Taft Benson, "To the 'Youth of the Noble Birthright,'" *Ensign*, May 1986, p. 43.

46. Ezra Taft Benson, "The Book of Mormon – Keystone of Our Religion," *Ensign*, November 1986, p. 7.

47. Marion G. Romney, "The Book of Mormon," *Ensign*, May 1980, p. 67.

48. *The Book of Mormon*, Introduction, Salt Lake City: The Church of Jesus Christ of Latter-day Saints, 1981.

49. Daniel H. Ludlow, "The Challenge of the Book of Mormon," *The Book of Mormon: The Keystone Scripture*," Paul R. Cheesman, ed., Religious Studies Center, Brigham Young University, p.20.